The Stages of Human Evolution: Human and Cultural Origins, second edition, C. *Loring Brace*

Tribesmen, *Marshall D. Sahlins*

The Hunters, second edition, *Elman R. Service*

Peasants, *Eric R. Wolf*

FOUNDATIONS OF MODERN ANTHROPOLOGY SERIES

Marshall D. Sahlins, *Editor*

PRENTICE-HALL, INC., Englewood Cliffs, New Jersey 07632

C. Loring Brace, University of Michigan

The Stages

Human Evolution

HUMAN AND CULTURAL ORIGINS

Second Edition

Library of Congress Cataloging in Publication Data

Brace, C. Loring.
    The stages of human evolution.

    (Foundations of modern anthropology series)
    Bibliography: p.
    Includes index.
    1.   Human evolution.   2.   Man, Prehistoric.
I. Title.
GN281.B67 1978   573'.3   78-18387
ISBN 0-13-840157-8
ISBN 0-13-840140-3 pbk.

To my parents, Professor and Mrs. Gerald W. Brace

Printed in the United States of America

10   9   8   7   6   5   4   3   2   1

PRENTICE-HALL
FOUNDATIONS OF MODERN ANTHROPOLOGY SERIES

Marshall D. Sahlins, Editor

PRENTICE-HALL INTERNATIONAL, INC., London
PRENTICE-HALL OF AUSTRALIA PTY. LIMITED, Sydney
PRENTICE-HALL OF CANADA, LTD., Toronto
PRENTICE-HALL OF INDIA PRIVATE LIMITED, New Delhi
PRENTICE-HALL OF JAPAN, INC., Tokyo
PRENTICE-HALL OF SOUTHEAST ASIA PTE. LTD., Singapore
WHITEHALL BOOKS LIMITED, Wellington, New Zealand

Foundations
of Modern Anthropology
Series

The *Foundations of Modern Anthropology Series* is a documentation of the human condition, past and present. It is concerned mainly with exotic peoples, prehistoric times, unwritten languages, and unlikely customs. But this is merely the anthropologist's way of expressing his concern for the here and now, and his way makes a unique contribution to our knowledge of what's going on in the world. We cannot understand ourselves apart from an understanding of *man*, nor our culture apart from an understanding of *culture*. Inevitably we are impelled toward an intellectual encounter with man in all his varieties, no matter how primitive, how ancient, or how seemingly insignificant. Ever since their discovery by an expanding European civilization, primitive peoples have continued to hover over thoughtful men like ancestral ghosts, ever provoking this anthropological curiosity. To "return to the primitive" just for what it is would be foolish; the savage is not nature's nobleman, and his existence is no halcyon idyll. For anthropology, the romance of the primitive has been something else: a search for the roots and meaning of ourselves—in the context of all mankind.

The series, then, is designed to display the varieties of man and culture and the evolution of man and culture. All fields of anthropology are relevant to the grand design and all of them—prehistoric archaeology, physical anthropology, linguistics, and ethnology (cultural anthropology)—are represented among the authors of the several books in the series. In the area of physical anthropology are books describing the early condition of humanity and the subhuman primate antecedents. The later development of man on the biological side is set out in the volume on races, while the archaeological accounts of the Old World and the New document development on the historical side. Then there are the studies of contemporary culture, including a book on how to understand it all—i.e., on ethnological theory—and one on language, the peculiar human gift responsible for it all. Main types of culture are laid out in "The Hunters," "Tribesmen," "Formation of the State," and "Peasants." Initiating a dialogue between contemplation of the primitive and the present, the volume on "The Present as Anthropology" keeps faith with the promise of anthropological study stated long ago by E. B. Tylor, who saw in it "the means of understanding our own lives and our place in the world, vaguely and imperfectly it is true, but at any rate more clearly than any former generation."

Looked at from this point of view, the Neanderthal and Pithecanthropus skulls stand like the piers of a ruined bridge which once continuously connected the kingdom of man with the rest of the animal world.

William J. Sollas

Preface

Of all the subjects that have provoked the play of human curiosity, our concern with our own prehistoric origins has few equals. At the same time, few subjects have been the target for so much unprofessional speculation; and while the present work aims at no reduction in the quantity of speculations (quite the reverse), it is the hope of the author that they can, technically at least, bear the label of *professional* speculations. Part of the reason for the less-than-abundant work on human origins is that, in this material world, it can produce little measurable gain. Physics can produce bigger and more expensive explosions, basic biology has its medical consequences, and such subjects as geology and economics contribute to our mineral and monetary well-being, but prehistoric anthropology can reveal only the humble nature of human beginnings, and thus has dubious value as a marketable commodity. Many have regarded it as an interesting hobby, but few have been tempted to treat it as a serious career and devote lifelong concentration to its advancement. Even among the professional practitioners, the competition to qualify is often less severe than is true for other fields, with the result that advances and accomplishments have been far less spectacular than has been the case with, for instance, genetics or electronics. The subject is fascinating, nevertheless, and, for the professionals, it is quite satisfying in and of itself. It is the purpose of the present volume to communicate a modicum of this interest to the reader young or old; perhaps to kindle the spark of what might grow to be another professional career; and to add a possible modifying influence, however minor, to the understandable human tendency to magnify our present accomplishments to the point where we are inclined to forget how precarious was the very existence of our predecessors until the recent past—and perhaps may again be in the immediate future.

C. *Loring Brace*

Contents

PART ONE *Discovering the Evidence*

One Interpreting Human Evolution

Few among the educated and no serious scholars doubt that *Homo sápiens* evolved by natural means from a creature which today would not be considered human. From this initial point of agreement, the thinking of those who are considered qualified to judge diverges to such a degree that many feel we do not have a basis which is adequate enough to warrant any interpretation at all. Yet schemes have been constructed which attempt to arrange the prehistoric evidence and account for the course of human evolution, and, in the pages that follow, the strengths and weaknesses of a number of these will be presented and discussed.

Since it is generally agreed that evolutionary thinking should be applied to the course of prehistoric human development, it would seem unnecessary at first glance to consider the nonevolutionary or even anti-evolutionary views of pre-Darwinian thought. Further investigation, however, reveals that the differences between several of the attitudes discernible at the present time can in part be traced to the lingering influence of a current of thought which has specific pre-Darwinian sources. Once this has been identified and the historical connections have been traced, then the reason for the differences

3

between the major opposing interpretations will become obvious and we shall have some basis for making a choice between them.

Interpretations of the human fossil record can be arranged along a spectrum between two polar and opposed approaches. At one extreme, there is the school which takes all the known hominid fossils, arranges them in a lineal sequence, and declares that this is the course which human evolution has pursued. On the other hand, there is the school which declares that the course of evolution is never in a straight, unbranching line—witness the diversity of related forms in the organic world today—and that one should expect to find branches and specializations among human fossils. This latter view tends to regard the differing fossil hominids as "specializations" away from the main line of human evolution which eventually became extinct without issue.

People invariably are fascinated by the investigation of the skeletons in their closets, and in the field of human evolution one could say that this is *literally* the case. This fascination has led many people, amateur and professional, to write about the human fossil record—people who have not been fully qualified and who have failed to perceive the nature of the two schemes just mentioned. As a result, many authors prefer a hazy middle ground, since they feel that both schemes have some merit, and the result is that only a few authors today represent the poles in fully developed form. In the first edition of this book, one of the extreme positions was specifically defended—the linear scheme mentioned above—not because there was conclusive proof for it, but in an effort to follow the principles expounded by the medieval logician, William of Occam, for whom the best explanation was always the simplest. At the time, it appeared that the complexities of the most widely accepted interpretive schemes were more a product of the minds of their advocates than they were the necessary result of the available facts. Simplification, however, can be pushed too far, and the discoveries of the last five years have clearly shown that a rigid unilinear interpretation is in fact an oversimplification.

More of this later, but first it should be instructive to sample the various other current views on the course of human evolution. First among these and generally regarded as most traditional is the view that the different forms in the human fossil record are the results of the adaptive radiation of the basic human line. At present, there are several versions being stressed: one which treats the entire human fossil record as a picture of divergent "specialized" lines, most of which became extinct without issue; another which concentrates on the earlier parts of the record where various "specializations" are supposed to have occurred; and finally one which concentrates on the latter part of the record where the Neanderthals are identified as "specializations" on their way to extinction. Running through all of these is the tendency to deny possible ancestral status to any fossil that differs from modern form to any marked extent. To some extent, then, these schemata focus more on how human evolution presumably did *not* occur than on trying to find out what was actually going on.

To understand these applications and the criticisms which can be made of them, it is first necessary to gain some sort of perspective of the time scale in question, the fossils concerned, and the principles involved. Briefly, it has become apparent that the span during which the events of human evolution have occurred was not just 300,000 or 800,000 years, as was once believed, but somewhere in the neighborhood of 3 million years in duration. Previous estimates were based largely upon guesswork involving sedimentation rates and strata thicknesses, but this recent reappraisal is derived from the work of geophysicists who have utilized the known and constant rate of decay of Potassium 40 into Argon. The Potassium-Argon (K/A) proportion in ancient volcanics is directly related to the length of time since they have cooled, and while there are many pitfalls connected with the use of this technique to date strata in the recent past (three million years is dewy fresh in the full perspective of geological time), it is becoming increasingly apparent that the duration of human existence has been sufficient that one need not invoke an unusual rate of evolution to account for all the changes which the human fossil record reveals.

The geological period during which human form did most of its evolving is called the Pleistocene, and it extended from about two million years ago to 10,000 years ago, if indeed it can properly be considered ended. The oldest of our close fossil relatives are found in the Pliocene some three million years ago and are referred to as Australopithecines. These flourish for a span of about two million years, during which time they display a diversity of size, form, and robustness that has been the subject of some vigorous scholarly disagreement. The size spectrum runs from the modern average for bulk and stature down to creatures only half as large. The earliest ones appear to be small and the most robust ones appear to be late, but it is abundantly clear that little ones continued to exist at the same time that the big ones flourished. Aside from cases where they differ in bulk, the most evident points of distinction between the Australopithecines and modern humans are in the head and face. Simply stated, the head is smaller—brain size is scarcely more than a third that of the modern mean—while the faces and teeth are enormous. At the moment, there is a healthy professional brawl going on over the relationship of the robust Australopithecines to the gracile ones, and the significance of both to the total picture of human evolution. A solution to the controversy will be suggested later on in this book, but for now this initial brief sketch is offered so that the reader will have some framework on which he can arrange the arguments that follow.

In the middle of the Pleistocene some half a million years ago, there is another cluster of hominid fossils which can be called Pithecanthropines. In the Upper Pleistocene immediately prior to the appearance of men of recognizably modern form, there is a fossil group which has been called the Neanderthals. To be sure, there are other fossils unevenly scattered, in both the geographical and temporal sense, which provide a source for much of the disagreement which still surrounds any attempt to develop a systematic view of human evolution; but the foregoing should provide a useful outline to remember while the discovery of the human fossil record is being recounted.

The scheme which will be developed in later chapters essentially takes these major blocks of fossil hominids, arranges them in temporal sequence, and explores the evolutionary logic whereby the earlier evolved into the later ones. It is these major groups which form the evolutionary stages through which it is claimed that the human line passed. Yet it should also be remembered that the identification of these supposed "stages" is largely dependent upon the accident of discovery. A few rich sites have provided concentrated evidence for particular forms of human fossils, and it is not only possible but extremely likely that had these rich sites involved different time levels, then the identification and number of important stages in human evolution would have been rather different. On the other hand, the present stages perceived are adequate to represent the changes involved, and their consideration can be justified in terms of their utility.

Ultimately, when the entire time spectrum of human existence is documented by an as-yet-unforeseeable abundance of fossil evidence, the picture should be one of a completely gradual continuum of accumulating change, with no visible breaks between what are here considered as stages. Human evolution has been continual; it continues in the present, and will continue in the future; but our concern in this book is the changes which have taken place in the past.

Two Fact and Fancy
before 1860

The earliest recognition of a fossil human was accorded a skull fragment discovered in the year 1700 at Canstatt, near Stuttgart in western Germany. At this early date, however, there was not even the remotest suspicion that modern living forms, including human ones, might have evolved by natural means from earlier forms ultimately quite different in appearance. Nor was there any faint hint of the vistas of geological antiquity which research was to reveal in the subsequent century. The Canstatt skull was accepted by some as evidence for human existence in ancient times, but its form was not different from that of modern human form, and "ancient times" were measured in terms of a total span since creation—thought to be somewhat less than 6,000 years. As late as the middle of the seventeenth century, the vision of such antiquity was considered somewhat daring, although it had received a certain amount of religious sanction in the work of the biblical scholar James Ussher, Archbishop of Armagh. Computing from the named generations recorded in the Bible, Ussher arrived at the conclusion that creation had occurred in the year 4004 B.C. To this, the Reverend Dr. John Lightfoot, vice-chancellor of Cambridge University, added the pronouncement that

7

". . . heaven and earth, centre and circumference, were created all together in the same instant, and clouds full of water. This work took place and man was created by the Trinity on October 23, 4004 B.C. at nine o'clock in the morning."

By the end of the eighteenth century, appraisals of geological processes and accumulating knowledge of the structure and strata of the earth led to the suspicion, on the part of some people, that the earth was really very much older. Fossil remains of extinct and different animals had been discovered, and scholars were becoming aware that the world had been a very different place in ages gone by, and that great changes had occurred. A few people even noted that the shaped pieces of flint discovered in prehistoric strata might be human tools made before the discovery of metallurgy, and certainly historians and students of human institutions were aware that the human world had changed even in the recent past.

Early in the nineteenth century, the French biologist Lamarck tried to promote a view that continuous and accumulating change was the normal state of affairs. He was really the first thoroughgoing evolutionist, but the mechanism which he proposed to account for organic change was incorrect and his position has been generally rejected. The initial reason for this rejection was the fact that many people were emotionally unprepared to accept change as normal. The traditional view that the world was created fixed and changeless had both social and religious support, and a scheme proposing the normality of constant change was regarded as a threat to the established order. Yet change could be seen in the geological record of the remote past, and some sort of explanation was demanded.

An acceptable solution was proposed by another French scholar, Georges Cuvier, who was a younger contemporary of Lamarck. Cuvier's scheme has been called catastrophism. It claimed that the various geological layers had been deposited as the result of a series of cataclysms which had overwhelmed the planet periodically, extinguishing all previously living organisms. The last of these cataclysms, according to Cuvier, was the Biblical flood, which meant that human remains should not be discoverable in previous layers. Cuvier is credited with the statement: "Fossil man does not exist." And indeed, in the early nineteenth century there was very little known evidence to contradict such a position.

Cuvier was somewhat vague concerning the origin of the new animals which appeared in the strata overlying his various supposed cataclysms. Not only did he suggest that they might have migrated into the area concerned from other parts of the world which had not been affected by the regional catastrophe, but he also gave support to a philosophy of successive creations. With the development of Darwinian evolutionary theory in the middle of the nineteenth century, the view of supernaturally caused extinctions, migrations, invasions, and successive creations was superseded as a general explanation. Yet, because of a variety of historical accidents, something of this has survived into the present, at least where considerations of human origins are concerned.

The discovery of the fossil and the archaeological evidence for human evolution was the result of the field work of people who had very little concern

Georges Cuvier (1769–1832), zoologist, comparative anatomist, paleontologist, and unwitting influence on many of the subsequent attempts to interpret the human fossil record. (Brown Brothers.)

for the research which developed the evolutionary explanation for the origin of organic diversity and organic change, yet both realms of activity have parallel careers extending back into the eighteenth century. Archaeological and paleontological work could and did go on without much concern for theoretical implications. Cuvier, in spite of being specifically opposed to evolution, can be regarded as the founder of paleontology, a discipline which, ironically, provides the most direct evidence in support of evolutionary theory. His intellectual descendants (and other unrelated antiquarians and archaeologists) pursued their diggings right up into the twentieth century, with often quite incorrect assumptions concerning their interpretations. Darwin, on the other hand, used relatively little paleontological evidence to support his major insights. This was partly because of the very incomplete nature of knowledge concerning the fossil record, and partly because his concern was focussed on the attempt to explain diversity in the world of *living* organisms.

Although it has remained for the twentieth century to attempt the thorough synthesis of these two areas of endeavor, scholars in both areas have not been unaware of the implications each has had for the other, and the public has been sensitive to this from the beginning. This still shows in the common misconception concerning the title of Darwin's most famous book, *On the Origin of Species*. From the time of its appearance right up to the present, people who are not thoroughly familiar with it have assumed that it suggests a common ancestry for apes and people, and that the "species" in the title refers to humanity itself. This latter assumption is so strong that the

9

title is frequently misquoted, being rendered as *The Origin of "The" Species*. Actually, only one brief sentence at the very end makes any reference to humans at all, and this is thoroughly noncommittal. Darwin's concern for human evolution was reserved for expression in another book, *The Descent of Man*, published more than a decade after his *Origin*. Even here, however, his reference to the skimpy fossil and archaeological record of human prehistoric existence is brief in the extreme.

The trickle of accumulating evidence had been growing, however, with prehistoric skeletons and stone tools being brought forth even during the lifetime of Cuvier. During the 1820's, human skeletal material was discovered in association with extinct animals and ancient stone tools on the coast of Wales, in France, and in Belgium, but none of it attracted much attention. Late in the 1840's Boucher de Perthes, a customs inspector at Abbeville in northwestern France, published the results of his prehistoric investigations of the previous 15 years. In the gravel of the Somme river terraces he had discovered flints of such a regular shape that they could only be the products of human manufacture. Yet they obviously were deposited during the course of the formation of the terraces where they were found, which suggested an age for their makers far in excess of anything granted by even the most liberal supporters of human antiquity.

Just a year later, in 1848, a skull was found in a quarry on the north face of the Rock of Gibraltar; this skull we now recognize as a representative of the Neanderthal stage of human evolution. The discovery was recorded by the Gibraltar Scientific Society. A slow 14 years later, after the skull had found its way to England, it was shown to at best mildly interested scholars at meetings of the British Association for the Advancement of Science, and at an anthropological congress. Just 20 years after its discovery it was presented, pretty much as a curiosity piece, to the Museum of the Royal College of Surgeons in London, where it remained, almost forgotten, until after the turn of the century. Since its importance went unappreciated for more than half a century following its exhumation, it played no part in the development of the study of human evolution, which is rather a pity since it differs markedly from the stereotype of the heavily buttressed, muscle-marked, and robust image that is conjured up in the minds of so many when the name Neanderthal is invoked.

Relegation to unimportant obscurity was very nearly the fate of the archaeological discoveries of Boucher de Perthes. Contemporary French scholars were so scornful of his claims that they never even bothered to visit his diggings or investigate his work firsthand, simply remaining in Paris and denouncing him from a distance. Had it not been for the curiosity of a group of English scientists, his finds would have had as little influence on the study of human origins as had the Gibraltar skull.

By a remarkable set of historical coincidences, the late 1850's saw the discovery of the skeletal remains of what could be identified as an earlier stage in human evolution, the recognition of the archaeological evidence for human antiquity, and the development of an intellectual framework within which these new facts could be encompassed. The specific timing of these events was a little less fortunate, since the discovery of the skeletal remains

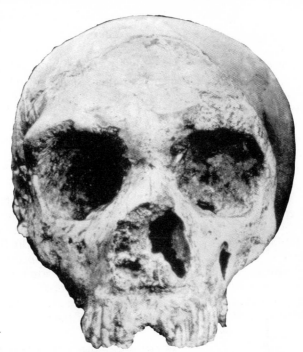

The Gibraltar discovery—a skull of Neanderthal form.

occurred first, and they were the subject of sceptical comments which have influenced interpretations ever since. The skeleton was discovered in 1856 during quarry operations in a limestone gorge through which flows the Dussel, a tributary of the lower Rhine. The gorge lies in the area between Elberfeld and Dusseldorf and bears the name of Neanderthal. By giving its name to the skeleton discovered there, it has provided a designation for the entire stage of evolutionary development immediately prior to the emergence of modern human form.

The skeleton had evidently been a burial in a small cave in the limestone cliffs, and had probably been complete. In the course of being recovered it was somewhat battered, since it, along with the dirt in which it lay, was unceremoniously shovelled out onto the terrace by quarry workers who were cleaning out the cave to get at the rock. Its human nature was later recognized by Johann Karl Fuhlrott, a natural science teacher at the high school in Elberfeld, who assured its preservation. Fuhlrott, with the aid of Hermann Schaaffhausen, a professor of anatomy at Bonn, promoted the view that this was an early form of man, but their interpretation received no support until very nearly the end of the nineteenth century. Possibly because of the mode of excavation, the face was not recovered—the head being represented by the skullcap from the ridges over the eye sockets on to the back of the skull but minus the base. The limb bones were extraordinarily robust and the brow ridges of the skull enormous, but, lacking the face, jaws, and teeth, the evidence for clear difference from modern form was subject to debate.

And debate there was. Enough peculiarities were present to suggest all sorts of explanations, from hints that it was an ancient Celt of "low type" similar to the modern Irish, to suggestions that it was an idiot, a freak, the victim of rickets, or the residue of the Mongolian Cossacks who had chased

11

Napoleon back from Russia in 1814. The most authoritative opinion was delivered by one of Germany's leading scientists, Rudolf Virchow, a founder of German anthropology and, as the originator of the field of cellular pathology, the most outstanding pathologist of the day. After careful examination, he pronounced it pathological and sought to explain all of its peculiarities in that fashion. The weight of his judgment has been such that Neanderthal morpohology has been regarded as "aberrant" from that day to this, and a majority of authorities even today refuse to accept Neanderthals as representative of the ancestors of modern human beings.

In 1858, the year following the first discussion of the Neanderthal discovery, a delegation from the Royal Society of Great Britain visited the excavations of Boucher de Perthes in northern France and returned, convinced of the significance of his work, to report to the British scientific world. Then, in 1859, Darwin's work *On the Origin of Species* appeared. From then on, human attitudes toward the world of nature and their own position within it were permanently altered. No longer could people regard themselves as the epitome of existence in a world created for their own benefit. Of course, for quite some time, in the pride of their self-importance, many people

Charles R. Darwin (1809–1882), author of *On the Origin of Species* and acknowledged father of evolutionary thinking. (National Portrait Gallery, London.)

could not accept the implications of this presentation. However, as time went on and acceptance became nearly universal, it became apparent that the consequent enforced humility was doing people no harm. The upshot of the entire matter is that no area of human behavior and philosophy has escaped the impact of the consequent revolution in attitudes.

Three The Pictur

Up to 190(

The vindication of Boucher de Perthes and the intellectual revolution going on in Britain could not fail to be a great stimulus to prehistoric research. During the late 1850's and 1860's, basic work on discovering the characteristics of human cultures prior to the existence of metal was undertaken. In France, particularly in the Dordogne region, and the Vézère river valley of the southwest, excavations at La Madeleine, Solutré, Aurignac, and Le Moustier revealed stone tool-making traditions. These were named Magdalenian, Solutrean, Aurignacian, and Mousterian and are now known to be roughly 20, 25, 30, and 40 thousand years old, respectively. It was suspected that these dated from a period more recent than those discovered by Boucher de Perthes, but no one then imagined that the difference was actually more than 100,000 years. Then, most exciting of all, in 1868, human skeletal remains were discovered in the same stratigraphic layer with tools of Aurignacian type. To the interest as well as the relief of the public, these remains indicated that the individuals in question were not markedly different from modern form. In fact, their appearance has been portrayed with a glowing enthusiasm not entirely warranted by their somewhat fragmentary condition.

14

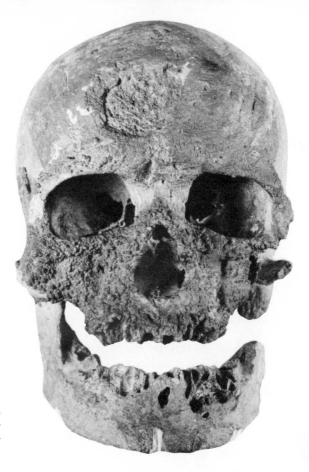

The male Cro-Magnon, from Les Eyzies, Dordogne, France. (Courtesy of the Musée de l'Homme, Paris.)

The human skeletal remains which we have been discussing, representing some five individuals, were discovered during the course of constructing the railroad through Les Eyzies, in the aforementioned Dordogne department of southwestern France. The removal of fill for the abutments of the railway bridge revealed a long-hidden rock shelter near an eminence called Cro-Magnon, within which the skeletons and artifacts were found. Competent geologists were on hand to verify the antiquity and the stratigraphic associations, and the study of human fossils was finally given its first solidly documented specimens. Stature of the male skeleton can be computed to be 5'10" or 5'11", which is tall in comparison to present or previous worldwide standards, and the rugged, long bones suggest a robust and muscular people. The face was vertical rather than projecting, and possessed a prominent chin, although these features have been stressed to a greater extent than the evidence warrants in light of the fact that the large male cranium was toothless at discovery.

Still, the Cro-Magnon finds were recognizably of modern form and provide the basis for the still valid assertion that the Upper Paleolithic toolmaking traditions—Aurignacian, Solutrean, Magdalenian, and others—were the products of people not unlike ourselves. Associated art work in the form of carvings and engravings on bone and ivory revealed a degree of sophisti-

15

cation in these Upper Pleistocene hunters which was quite gratifying from the point of view of the people who were beginning to accept these Upper Palaeolithic people as ancestral to more recent humanity. The decades which followed witnessed the discovery of abundant additional support for the picture outlined in the discoveries at Cro-Magnon, and it was some time before the unearthing of more ancient remains again forced people to face the issues of human evolution—the possibility that humans had arisen from something quite different from their present form.

Exactly 30 years after the original discovery in the Neanderthal, and long enough for the controversy to have died down, two human skeletons were found buried in a Mousterian level in a cave in the commune of Spy (pronounced Spee) in the province of Namur, Belgium. The form of both skeletons was recognizably similar to that of the original Neanderthal, and the skull Spy I was of practically the identical shape. No longer was it possible to expound with such certainty the supposed pathological features of the individual from the Neanderthal. However, the adamant Virchow refused to back down and, although the Spy discoveries confirmed the Neanderthal as a valid human type, the implications of abnormality and peculiarity tended to remain; indeed, to this day they have not been fully shaken off. Nevertheless, the Neanderthals could now be regarded as a type, associated with a definite tool-making tradition, and given a definite age.

The scene was shortly to shift to another part of the world and involve another, and possibly even more dramatic, form of human fossil. The German naturalist Ernst Haeckel, greatly excited by the implications of Charles Darwin's work, was communicating his enthusiasm for the evolutionary viewpoint to a rising generation of students on the German academic scene. Pushing evolutionary logic to its conclusion, Haeckel drew a hypothetical family tree linking modern man to a common ancestry with the living apes and monkeys. He further suggested that somewhere in between the two, back in the remote past, there must have been a form which was neither one nor the other—a completely transitional stage. This he suggested should be referred to as *Pithecanthropus alalus*, i.e., ape-man without speech. An American journalist was later to christen this the "missing link," a term which remains as a firm item of popular folklore. Whereas Darwin had suggested that Africa was the most likely place to search for the earliest human ancestor, believing that the gorilla and the chimpanzee were our closest living relatives, Haeckel and others in Germany stressed Southeast Asia, since they claimed that the detailed morpohology of the gibbon's skull was more akin to the human than was that of the African anthropoid apes. Today, it appears that Darwin's suspicions were the sounder, although the discoveries of the 1890's made Haeckel's guess seem little short of inspired.

Fascinated by Haeckel's hypothetical portrayal of human ancestry, one of his former students, a young Dutch doctor named Eugene Dubois, went forth with the avowed intention of finding the "missing link." At the time this seemed like the most hare-brained thing in the world to do, since he had to give up a promising career as a teacher of anatomy at Amsterdam, and since there was virtually no shred of evidence in support of his scheme. Nevertheless, fortune smiled on Dubois and, by a piece of impossibly good luck, he did indeed find what he was looking for. As an indication of the improbability of his venture, the only other instance where an expedition set out with the deliberate intent of finding early man yielded the discovery of dinosaur eggs.

Plagued by a lack of funds—his project sounded so absurd that no one was willing to back him—Dubois signed up as a health officer in the Dutch colonial forces in what is now Indonesia. He was first assigned to Sumatra, where he spent several years hunting fossils. A variety of circumstances led him to suspect that Java was a more likely area, and in 1889 he got himself transferred there. He remained in Java for the next five years, and there made the discoveries for which he will always be remembered. In 1890 he discovered a small fragment of a lower jaw whose importance was only recognized later. In 1891 his excavations unearthed a skullcap with such a low forehead and heavy brow ridge, and with such marked constriction between the brow and the brain case, that he attributed it to a chimpanzee. In 1892, some 50 feet away from the skull in the same layer, he found a thighbone (femur) which was practically indistinguishable from the femur of modern man. This he claimed belonged to the individual represented by the skull, and for a while believed that he had discovered an erect walking chimpanzee. Comparative studies and measurements forced him to alter his opinion, since the skull, however primitive or ape-like in form, was halfway between that of a man and that of a chimpanzee in gross size, possessing a brain which fell within the lower limits of the normal modern range of variation. This he realized was his missing link, but (in contrast to the semi-erect posture which had been attributed to the Spy and Neanderthal finds) it was an erect walking missing link. So he slightly modified Haeckel's designation and, in his monograph of 1894, christened his discovery *Pithecanthropus erectus*. This still serves as the type specimen for our Pithecanthropine stage, although it is no longer regarded as a separate genus.

Dubois' admirable monograph created an international sensation and, when he returned to Europe in 1895, he was an immediate celebrity. The International Zoological Congress met at Leyden in 1895, where Dubois and his Pithecanthropus were the focus of attention of an unparalleled gathering of famous scholars. After prolonged argument, three schools of thought emerged.[1] One, siding with Dubois, felt that Pithecanthropus was neither an ape nor a human, but a genuine transitional form.[2] Another felt that it was on the human side of the boundary—primitive, perhaps, but hominid nevertheless.[3] The third group, headed by the aged Virchow, regarded it as being a giant form of gibbon, interesting and unusual, but only an ape after all. The controversy continued unresolved for many years, and it was not until the late 1920's and 1930's, when more Pithecanthropine skeletal remains were discovered in China near Peking, and also in Java, that general acceptance was possible. The Chinese Pithecanthropines, originally christened *Sinanthropus pekinensis* in 1927, were associated with stone tools and ancient hearths, which confirmed the implications of the human status of the Pithecanthropines as a whole. Paradoxically, among the very few voices now raised in opposition to the human status of *Pithecanthropus* was that of the elderly Dubois himself. Although he was willing to accept the new discoveries of Java and China as genuine early human beings, he reverted to, and for

the last 20 years of his life professed, the opinion voiced by Virchow in 1895
(that his original Pithecanthropus was actually a giant gibbon) and would
not accept the new Java and China finds as Pithecanthropines—as descendants of what he now considered were not even transitional ape-men, but
apes.

While full confirmation for the significance of *Pithecanthropus* had to wait
some 30 years, most scholars at and following the turn of the century came
to feel that it could be regarded as an extremely primitive form of humanity.
What with Pithecanthropines, Neanderthals, and moderns established at different times, and at least the latter two associated with different archaeological traditions, it was possible, during the first years of the twentieth century,
to suggest a logical evolutionary scheme containing all the known human
fossils arranged in terms of relationships and chronology. This was done by
Gustav Schwalbe, professor of anatomy at the University of Strassburg, who
capped a series of papers and monographs of the late nineteenth and early
twentieth centuries with his summary work, *Studies on the Prehistory of
Man*, published in 1906. In this he tentatively proposed a picture of the evolutionary history of man comprising three successive stages—Pithecanthropus,
Neanderthal, and Modern—allowing for the possibility of adjustments and
modifications which future finds would make inevitable.

Gustav Schwalbe
(1844–1916), Strass-
burg anatomist and
physical anthropologist,
who first arranged the
known human fossils in
an evolutionary se-
quence. (Courtesy
Ashley Montagu.)

Schwalbe's scheme was useful, flexible, and in accord with the evidence available at that time. With one major addition, it proved valuable enough to provide the organizing principle behind the interpretations offered in the later chapters of this book, although, for reasons which will be considered in the pages that follow, it has been generally rejected and forgotten by the anthropological world.

Four Homini[
Catastrophis[

In 1907, the year following Schwalbe's summary, a brief wave of excitement surrounded the discovery of an enormous mandible in a gravel pit near the village of Mauer, not far from the city of Heidelberg in western Germany. Without the rest of the skull, interpretations were somewhat inhibited, although the primitive characteristics were obvious. Still, the stratigraphy was precisely documented, indicating that the Heidelberg jaw was, as it remains today, among the oldest of the human fossils discovered in western Europe, being a probable representative of the Pithecanthropines. Certainly it was a contemporary of those Far Eastern specimens that have given us our most detailed knowledge of the appearance of the Pithecanthropine stage of human evolution.

In 1908, however, the scene of discovery shifted and the tide of historical accident began which is so largely responsible for the present interpretations of human evolution in general and of the Neanderthals in particular. At Le Moustier in southwestern France—the same village which gave its name to the tool-making tradition associated with the Neanderthals—a genuine Neanderthal burial was discovered. For a variety of reasons (initially related to

20

the somewhat dubious activities of the discoverer, a Swiss antiquities dealer who had been looting French archaeological sites and selling the booty to the highest bidder) the description was delayed for many years, and as a result the Le Moustier skeleton never played the role it deserved.

To make up for this, later in the same year and not far from the same region in southwestern France, another and more complete Neanderthal skeleton was discovered in excavations near the village of La Chapelle-aux-Saints. These remains were entrusted to Marcellin Boule, paleontologist at the National Museum of Natural History in Paris. During the next five years he produced a series of scholarly papers, climaxed by a massive monograph in three installments, appearing in 1911, 1912, and 1913. Boule's portrayal of this, the most complete Neanderthal skeleton yet discovered, formed the basis for the caricature of the cave man espoused by an entire subsequent generation of cartoonists, journalists, and, alas, professional scholars. The "Old Man" of La Chapelle-aux-Saints was depicted as being a creature structurally intermediate between modern man and the anthropoid apes.

The great toe was presumed to diverge, hinting that it still preserved a degree of opposability to the other toes, and, in doing so, it forced the possessors to walk on the outer margins of the feet in the awkward manner of the modern orang. Details of the knee joint were taken to indicate that it could not be entirely extended, meaning that the Neanderthals were not completely erect and could do no better than to shuffle along with a "bent-knee gait." This also was supposed to indicate their similarity to modern apes, although since apes are perfectly capable of fully extending their legs, such claims demonstrate an ignorance of the anatomy and functioning of the knee joint in both apes and humans. The same issues had been raised concerning the Spy skeletons, and several detailed studies before the end of the nineteenth century demonstrated how inapplicable they were, but Boule chose to ignore these. In harmony with the semi-erect picture conjured up by his discussion of the feet and legs, Boule claimed that the reverse curves present in the human neck and lower back were absent, as in the modern apes, and that the whole trunk indicated a powerful but incompletely upright postural adaptation. On top of his scarcely human caricature was a head which hung forward instead of being balanced on top of the spinal column. A detailed study of a cast made of the interior of the braincase convinced him that the brain was inferior in organization to that of modern man, particularly in the frontal lobes which, since the days when phrenology was respectable, everyone knew to be related to the higher functionings of the mind.

The significance of a continued and repeated use of words such as "ape-like," "primitive," and "inferior" was not lost on the fascinated public, which quickly invested the Neanderthals with a veritable hairy pelt and long simian arms, although there is no evidence whatever concerning hair and the arms were actually relatively short. In the years since that time, it has been demonstrated that Boule was in error on each one of the foregoing points, but the vision of the totality has not been altered and the Neanderthals continue to shuffle through the pages of numberless books and slouch stupidly in countless cartoons.

Having produced this caricature, Boule then proclaimed that it could have nothing to do with the ancestors of modern *Homo sapiens*. As justification, he claimed that the Neanderthals and their culture came to an abrupt end and were suddenly replaced by full *Homo Sapiens*, sweeping into Europe with their superior Upper Palaeolithic technology. Furthermore, said he, people of modern form already existed during the time when the Neanderthals were the main occupants of the European scene. This latter claim has provided one of the main stimuli for subsequent activities in human paleontology, since within a year Boule's candidate for this ancient modern was disqualified. From that time on, an entire generation of anthropologists has been searching for the as-yet-undiscovered *sapiens* in the Middle Pleistocene or even earlier.

Within the same year that the final installment of Boule's ponderous work appeared, an ingenious Englishman fabricated the famous Piltdown fraud which confused the picture for a full 40 years before being exposed. Piltdown turned out to be fragments of a modern human cranium and part of the jaw of a modern female orang, stained to look ancient, appropriately broken and artificially worn, and mingled with a collection of extinct animal bones acquired from all over the world before being scattered in a gravel pocket in southeastern England. Also, in the same year, Gustav Schwalbe published a review of Boule's monograph which, at 80 pages, was nearly a book in itself. In this he yielded to the picture painted by Boule and abandoned his own former claims that the Neanderthals were the direct ancestors of modern human beings, although he noted the evidence contradicting Boule's claim of ancient moderns. Schwalbe never abandoned Pithecanthropus, which he continued to regard as ancestral to all later human forms, although Boule had indicated that he considered *both* Neanderthal and Pithecanthropus to be branches off to the side of the mainstream of human evolution—branches which became extinct without issue.

In 1914, the year after Boule's publication, the First World War burst upon Europe. The dislocation of human affairs and the cessation of scholarly activity are inevitable companions of war, but in the field which pursues the study of human evolution, the legacy of this conflict has been more enduring if less clearly appreciated. Germany not only lost the war, but suffered a blow to her intellectual prestige which has had repercussions ever since. In the postwar era, Germany's intellectual recovery was progressively stifled by the rise of the Hitler regime which, when it came to power, quickly extinguished what had managed to survive. This was particularly true for any science which attempted to make an objective and unbiased study of human beings. Anthropology and the other social sciences suffered severely and have seen few contributions made and have played but a minor role in the general advances made in other countries. Little remains of the pre-World War I tradition in German anthropology and, while I can hear my colleagues muttering that this is really a good thing, the valuable parts have been eliminated along with the bad ones. It is to be regretted, for instance, that so little is remembered of the pre-Boule writings of Gustav Schwalbe.

Before proceeding, it should be interesting to consider briefly the source of Boule's orientation. Boule was a paleontologist, trained during the 80's

Aleš Hrdlička (1869–1943). Born in Czechoslovakia, raised in the United States, he was the first physical anthropologist at the Smithsonian Institution and one of the most distinguished representatives of the field in America. Hrdlička was one of the very few scholars after the First World War who continued to view the Neanderthals as a stage in human evolution [See his *The Skeletal Remains of Early Man*, 1930. (Courtesy of the Smithsonian Institution.)]

of the previous century in an academic environment which had not accepted the Darwinian view of evolution. Although French paleontologists spoke of "evolution," they carefully distinguished it from "Darwinism." To them, evolution signified the appearance of successive organic forms, whereas "Darwinism" meant the development of later forms out of earlier ones by natural processes, and this they refused to accept. When questioned concerning the source of the successive forms, they would evoke extinctions followed by invasions from elsewhere, and, ultimately, successive creations. This, then, was simply the survival of Cuvier's "catastrophism," re-labeled "evolution," and this was what Marcellin Boule applied to the human fossil record. As he noted, modern-looking humans appeared more recently than Neanderthals, so, following the tradition in which he was trained, he postulated Neanderthal extinction and subsequent modern invasion. This of course presupposed the existence of modern forms elsewhere, about which he, like Cuvier a century before, was relatively vague, and which has caused his followers a considerable degree of mental anguish ever since.

This view can be labeled hominid catastrophism, and, because of the historical accidents of the second decade of the present century, it has continued to dominate interpretations of human evolution, although it appears in a variety of forms and has been substantially modified. Following the First World War, Boule treated the totality of the known fossil record, presenting his scheme of hominid catastrophism—labeled "evolution"—in a single volume, *Fossil Men*. This book has continued to influence the field; an edition revised after Boule's death by a former student still remains as one of the few summary treatments.

23

Five Between

World War

During the course of the years, far more fossils have been discovered than there is room even to begin to record in a treatment as brief as this. Some of these, relatively important specimens, must be omitted because they have not met the criterion of contributing substantially to alterations in the over-all picture. The next discovery which did measure up was made in 1924; although it was but a little fossil for which only modest claims were made, in retrospect it can be regarded as a major portent of what was to come.

The scene was South Africa, where a small fossil skull was given to Raymond Dart, the young professor of anatomy at the medical school of the University of the Witwatersrand in Johannesburg. Dart had recently finished his training in medicine, anatomy, and physical anthropology in London, and was keenly aware that Africa, cited by Darwin as the possible source for the human line of development, had up to that time yielded no dated early human material at all. Only the single enigmatic and undated find of a Neanderthal-like skull in a mine shaft at Kabwe (then Broken Hill) in Zambia (formerly Northern Rhodesia) existed to demonstrate the presence of an earlier stage in human evolution. The little skull handed to Dart was that of an immature individual—approximately at the same stage of development as that of a modern six-year-old child—and it is a risky business to establish taxonomic affinity or evolutionary stage on the basis of specimens in which growth has not been completed. Still, Dart's study, published early in 1925, was able to demonstrate that his juvenile creature had a brain the size of a large adult gorilla, that its head was balanced atop the spinal column instead of slung forward, that the palate was human rather than ape-like in shape, and that, despite the great size of the teeth, the canines did not project beyond the level of the other teeth. Although he correctly noted that juvenile apes are less distinct from juvenile humans in some of these features than is the case where comparisons are made between adults of various forms, he could state in summary that this South African fossil, blasted out of a quarry at Taung, presented a curious mixture of ape-like and human features. Withal he regarded it as an extinct ape—closer perhaps to the human line than any yet discovered, but an ape nevertheless—and christened it *Australopithecus africanus* (Southern ape of Africa).

Dart's sober and relatively cautious appraisal was greeted by an outburst of patronizing scorn from the evolutionary and anatomical authorities back in England, several of whom were his former teachers. Chief among these was Sir Arthur Keith, champion of the Piltdown fraud, who repeatedly stated that Dart's position was "preposterous." In fairness it should be pointed out that Keith was in no way to be blamed for the fraudulent facets of the Piltdown melange, since he was as badly—even tragically—misled by

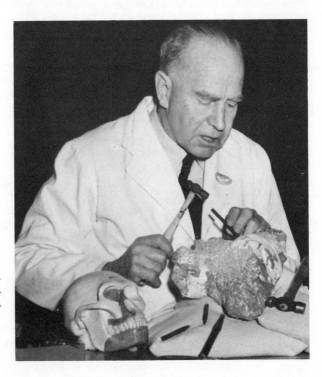

Raymond A. Dart, whose prophetic interpretation of *Australopithecus* went unappreciated for more than thirty years. (Photo courtesy of Professor Raymond Dart.)

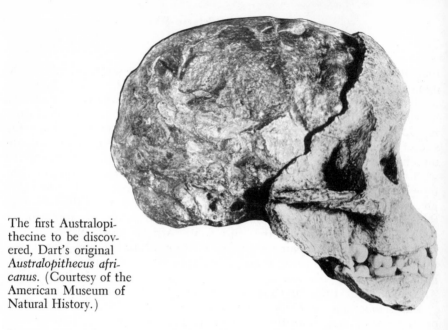

The first Australopi-
thecine to be discov-
ered, Dart's original
*Australopithecus afri-
canus.* (Courtesy of the
American Museum of
Natural History.)

it as anyone. Yet of all the criticism offered of Dart's views, only a relatively
trivial one remains, and this concerns the fact that he mixed terms of Latin
and Greek origin and used a substantive in place of an adjectival form in
assigning the fossil its name.

There seem to have been two sources for the reaction to Dart's claims.
One was the feeling that the fossil should really have been turned over to
the "proper authorities" (those back in England) for study. The second was
based on the feeling that, with Pithecanthropus finally accepted as the earliest
possible form of man, anything demonstrably more primitive, as *Australopithecus* was, even had it grown to adulthood, could not conceivably belong
in the picture. Influenced by such considerations, "Dart's child," as *Australopithecus* was deprecatingly referred to, was relegated to the category of "just
another fossil ape."

The excitement over Australopithecus was soon superseded by the discovery of Pithecanthropines in China, the so-called *Sinanthropus* remains or
Pekin man. During the succeeding decade, fragments of more than 40 individuals were retrieved from the limestone caves of Choukoutien, only a few
miles southwest of Pekin. Ultimately these were the subject of a series of
masterly monographs by Franz Weidenreich, a refugee from Hitler's Germany and, by great good fortune, one of the very few who perpetuated the
thinking of his late teacher and colleague, Gustav Schwalbe. War, with its
inevitable disrupting influence, spelled final oblivion from the original Sinanthropus material, which was last seen on December 7, 1941, when the out-
break of war in the Pacific caught them at Chin Wang Tao, the port of
embarkation, on the verge of being shipped to the United States for safe-
keeping. No trace of them has since been found, but, during their brief
resurrection, excellent casts were made and they were drawn, photographed,
and exhaustively described in Weidenreich's splendid publications. If any
doubt had remained concerning the human status of the Pithecanthropines,
it was now dispelled.

26

Franz Weidenreich (1873–1948) shown with Dr. G. H. R. von Koenigswald. (Courtesy of the American Museum of Natural History.)

The 1930's also saw important discoveries in other parts of the world. A skull from Steinheim in Germany (1933) and the back of a skull from Swanscombe in England (1935 and 1936) partially serve to fill the long gap between the time of the Pithecanthropines and that of the Neanderthals, although their interpretation is still the subject of prolonged debate. More important, however, were discoveries made in the Middle East and again in South Africa. The Middle Eastern finds were the result of excavations on the slopes of Mount Carmel, in Israel (then Palestine), a little more than a mile from the shores of the Mediterranean. There, in the years 1931 and 1932, a joint Anglo-American archaeological expedition discovered the remains of at least a dozen fossil humans in two different caves. The one complete skeleton from the cave of Tabūn was of a female which was in other respects indistinguishable from the classic Neanderthals of Europe. This at least demonstrated that the Neanderthals were not a limited European phenomenon. This point was also demonstrated by the simultaneous discovery of a series of skulls, approaching Pithecanthropine form but still within the Neanderthal spectrum, in Java, only 20 miles downstream from Trinil, where the original Pithecanthropus had been found. Recently, more full Neanderthals have been found at Shanidar cave in northern Iraq, again attesting to Neanderthal distribution.

The second Palestinian cave, Mugharet es-Skhūl, divulged the remains of at least 10 individuals, but rather than exhibiting fully Neanderthal form,

27

they displayed characteristics which were halfway between Neanderthal and Modern. This has earned them the designation of "Neanderthaloid"—that is, recalling the Neanderthals on the one hand, but not to a sufficient degree to separate them from modern man on the other. By one of those little ironies which only fate can arrange, the major burden of description and interpretation fell to Sir Arthur Keith. He who had been so critical of Dart's attempt to make sense out of a mixture of simian and human traits was now confronted with the task of interpreting a mixture of Neanderthal and modern ones, and his vacillations between alternate possibilities satisfied no one. Opinion tended to regard both Mount Carmel sites as third interglacial, i.e., before the fourth and last Pleistocene ice advance and therefore before the time of the European Neanderthals. Such being the case, Tabūn was reasonable enough, but Skhūl remained a dilemma. Keith faced the problem squarely but could not decide whether Skhūl indicated the hybridization of a fully Neanderthal population (represented by Tabūn) and the long-sought but as-yet-undiscovered modern one, or whether it was a Neanderthal population in the throes of rapid evolutionary change in the direction of modern man. He seemed to favor the latter explanation, although others have stressed the former. In any case, the issue has been drastically changed by recent refinements in dating which have removed both Mount Carmel sites from the third interglacial. It now appears that Tabūn is about 60,000 years old, which makes it a contemporary of full Neanderthals elsewhere, while Skhūl is around 35,000 years old, being halfway between proper Neanderthals and accepted moderns in both appearance and date.

Because of the dating difficulties, the Mount Carmel problem remained unsolved for a full 30 years. Meanwhile, in 1936, old issues of another sort were reopened, and this time the evidence was sufficient to ward off attempts to sweep them under the rug. Just when it seemed that the furor over Dart's *Australopithecus* had been reduced to a memory, another fortunate explosion

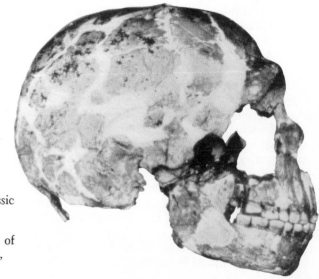

The skull of a classic
Neanderthal woman
from the cave of
et-Tabūn. (Courtesy of
the Clarendon Press,
Oxford.)

occurred. This particular blast took place in a limeworks quarry at Sterkfontein, some miles north of Johannesburg in the Transvaal area of South Africa. Fossil bones were discovered as a result and, by good fortune, were delivered into the hands of the venerable vertebrate paleontologist Robert Broom. Fragments of nearly half a dozen creatures were included, among them a complete adult skull. Broom immediately recognized the similarity of these to *Australopithecus*—eventually he advocated an entire taxonomic subfamily, the Australopithecinae, to include them all—but he believed that the new finds were different enough to warrant new generic and specific designations. He called them *Pleisianthropus transvaalensis*. Time has shown that they are simply adult versions of *Australopithecus*, and so, for the present at least, they will simply be referred to as the early Australopithecines.

The upright carriage of the head and the extraordinarily human appearance of the distal end of a femur contributed to the suspicion that these creatures may have been erect walking bipeds, and it began to appear as though Dart had not been so rash as his detractors had claimed. Nor was this all. Two years later, in 1938, on a farm named Kromdraai some two miles from Sterkfontein, more Australopithecine remains were discovered and brought to the attention of Robert Broom. Fragments of skull, jaw, teeth, arm, hand, and foot bones suggested a similar but more robust creature, which Broom called *Paranthropus robustus* and which we shall refer to en masse as the late or robust Australopithecines.

Now, with the weight of Broom's years of paleontological experience and the quantity of accumulating evidence, the Australopithecines could no longer be passed off as figments of a youthful fancy. However, consistent with the principles of hominid catastrophism, modified or extreme, and convinced that men of modern form would yet be discovered in the early Pleistocene, most anthropologists supported the view that the Australopithecines were simply another side branch from the main stem of human evolution and had become extinct without issue. To be sure, a few anthropologists, notably the American student of the Neanderthals, Hrdlička, and Franz Weidenreich, complained that the human evolutionary tree portrayed by most scholars was in effect all branches and no trunk, but real qualms did not develop until after the Second World War.

With the close of the 1930's, war came to the West and, as invariably happens under such circumstances, fossil hunting ceased and evolutionary studies were seriously impeded. Fortunately, the conflagration was delayed a while in the Far East, and work continued for a time in China and Java. The last major find of the prewar era in the East was made by the Dutch paleontologist G. H. R. von Koenigswald, who had been responsible for further Pithecanthropine finds in Java throughout the late 1930's. Just before the Japanese occupation in 1941, he found a small fragment of a rugged mandible with a few large but clearly human teeth to which he gave the relatively jawbreaking name, *Meganthropus palaeojavanicus*. A similar mandible was found in the same area in 1952, and for a while some anthropologists thought that these belonged to a genuine Australopithecine. This, if true, would be the only example of an Australopithecine outside of Africa and therefore of extraordinary significance. The material is really too skimpy for a definitive diagnosis, but using what is available, comparative analysis shows that it cannot be distinguished from robust Pithecanthropine form. It is considerably earlier in date than the Middle Pleistocene Pithecanthropines from China and elsewhere in Java, and its robustness could well be an indication that it is closer in form as well as in time to the Australopithecine ancestors wherever they might have been.

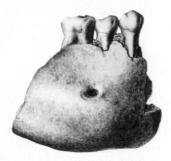

"Meganthropus palaeojavanicus," a robust Pithecanthropine from the early Pleistocene of Java. (Courtesy of Dr. G. H. R. von Koenigswald.)

Dr. Robert Broom (1866–1951), physician and paleontologist, with a cast of Pleisianthropus. (Courtesy of the American Museum of Natural History.)

Six Recent

Discoveries

In 1947, soon after peace made it possible once again to return to his pre-historic research, Dr. Broom, now more than 80 years of age but undiminished in energy, resumed his investigations of Sterkfontein. Within a short time he discovered quantities of Australopithecine remains, among which was a nearly complete half pelvis. This bone was remarkably like the pelvis of modern man and, of all the Australopithecine fragments found to date, most clearly demonstrated their erect and bipedal mode of locomotion. Yet tradi-tional anthropological doubts were raised, and it was hinted by some that perhaps the pelvic fragment properly belonged to the long-sought true man and had nothing to do with Australopithecines. Variants of this argument continue to be offered concerning other fragments of evidence but, like the cry of "pathological" which was repeatedly applied to early human fossils in the late nineteenth century, this has begun to sound more than a little strained.

The year 1947 also saw the return of Raymond Dart to the arena of Aus-tralopithecine research. His work was concentrated on a deserted lime-works dump at Makapansgat, some 200 miles northeast of Sterkfontein. This dump

31

produced a wealth of Australopithecine fragments, evidently of the same sort of those of Taung and Sterkfontein, although Dart gave them a new specific name. Within two years Dart had also recovered substantial fragments of pelvis which, if anything, were even more manlike than those from Sterkfontein. Also in 1947, Sir Arthur Keith published a handsome and gracious apology, noting that it was he who had been rash and hasty in 1925 and that time and events had proven Dart's interpretation to be much more nearly correct than his own.

Starting in the succeeding year, 1948, Broom and his assistant, J. T. Robinson, began work at another site, Swartkrans, a short distance from Sterkfontein, where they soon found Australopithecines of the same sort that Broom had found at Kromdraai 10 years before. Adding still another dimension to the early Pleistocene fossil picture as seen in the Transvaal of South Africa, a pocket in the Swartkrans site produced another form of human fossil. The first fragment, a nearly complete jaw found in 1949, was initially given the name of *Telanthropus capensis*, but comparative study has convinced Robinson and others that it is not distinguishable from the Pithecanthropines of Asia. As such, it is a find of the greatest significance. Dart and his assistants at Makapansgat and, following Broom's death in 1951, Robinson at Swartkrans and Sterkfontein, continued to recover fossil fragments of various kinds during the succeeding decade.

The three decades since the end of the Second World War have seen the discovery of human fossil material from all corners of the world, representing all stages of human evolution. Some, such as the extensive Neanderthal discoveries at Shanidar cave in northern Iraq (starting in 1953), and Pithecanthropine material from Tautavel (Arago) in the French Pyrenees, are of major significance, but so far the finds from sub-Saharan Africa have not yielded the center of the stage. The scope of this book does not allow me to indulge in the treatment of more than a fraction of these fascinating finds, although I must confess that my enthusiasm is in no way reduced by finding myself confined to the discoveries of greatest dramatic import.

The final facet of this historical review will be concerned with the East African discoveries initiated by the work of Dr. and Mrs. L. S. B. Leakey at Olduvai Gorge, Tanganyika (now Tanzania). While the finds which made them famous did not begin to occur until 1959, the basis which makes these discoveries so important goes back more than a third of a century to the time when Dr. Leakey first started making expeditions to this area. His general experience in East African prehistory goes back even further, but he first visited Olduvai Gorge in 1931 and shortly thereafter discovered tools of a type as crude as or cruder than those of any known tradition. Because of their location, these have been called Oldowan tools; they are now regarded as constituting the oldest tool-making tradition in the world. The Leakeys' continued work in Olduvai Gorge has revealed the development of the Oldowan tradition through the ascending layers until it becomes the familiar "hand-axe" tradition recognized a century ago by Boucher de Perthes at Abbeville and widely distributed throughout the Middle Pleistocene of the Old World. Here, then, is the Lower Pleistocene parent of the hand-axe and, by extension, the Lower Pleistocene parent of all subsequent human cultural traditions including our own—a confirmation of Darwin's prediction made so long ago!

As if this were not enough of a contribution to have made during a lifetime, the Leakeys' continued persistence in the face of formidable financial and environmental obstacles has finally rewarded them with the discovery of the manufacturer of the Oldowan tools—the bones of what must be our own ancestors. On July 17, 1959, they discovered their first fossil "man." Although they followed the confusing paleontological practice of giving it a new generic and specific name, *Zinjanthropus boisei*, it turns out to be nothing less than an Australopithecine—one of the later, robust kinds—in spite of a number of relatively minor features cited as being distinctive.

Furthermore, the stratum could be dated by the Potassium-Argon (K/Ar) technique and this showed that robust or "Zinj" type Australopithecines existed in Africa 1.75 million years ago. Analysis of animal bones at this and many other sites, including those in the Transvaal of South Africa, suggests that the robust Australopithecines at Swartkrans were roughly contemporaneous with those at Olduvai Gorge.

The discovery of "Zinj" attracted worldwide attention and financial support and initiated a new era in human paleontology. Within just a few years, Dr. and Mrs. Leakey had uncovered the remains of gracile Australopithecines as well as Pithecanthropines at various levels in Olduvai Gorge. Although their work has been of the greatest value to students of human evolution, it has not been an unmixed blessing. Underlying Dr. Leakey's many productive years in the field was the unshaken conviction that nothing so crude

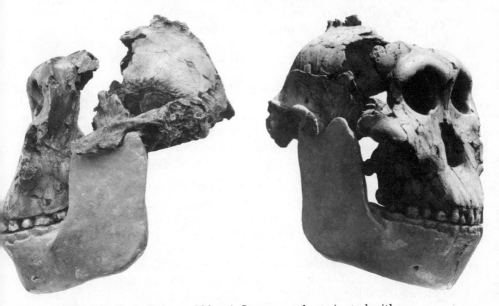

The "Zinj" skull from Olduvai Gorge, a robust Australopithecine, with an artist's idea of what the mandible should look like. (Photo by R. I. M. Campbell, Nairobi, Kenya.)

Olduvai Gorge, Tanzania. (Courtesy George H. Hansen.)

as an Australopithecine could possibly have been ancestral to subsequent human forms. He seemed to feel that the only proper ancestor for modern humanity was ancient "true man," and each new discovery was hailed as evidence for this patently nonevolutionary view until proper comparative study showed it to be one or another already known taxon. At one point, Dr. Leakey assembled a mixed collection of Australopithecine and Pithecanthropine material from Olduvai and tried to claim that this, which he called *"Homo habilis,"* (handy or skillful man), was the true human ancestor.

At the time of the first edition of this book, I had felt that, since the Australopithecines evolved straight into the Pithecanthropines, the two could not have been present at the same time. Each new piece of evidence that Leakey produced always turned out to have some flaw, and I rather equated his actions with those of the little boy who cried wolf. One of my colleagues reminded me, however, that in the old didactic story, eventually there was a wolf. And so there is in this case.

Dr. Leakey's richly productive life ended in 1972, by which time he had seen the fruitful beginnings of the continuation of his work by his son, Richard, in a promising area just east of Lake Turkana (then Lake Rudolf) in northern Kenya not far from the Ethiopian border. At that time, Richard Leakey's field crew had found a skull that was not quite a Pithecanthropine but was certainly tending in that direction. This, the cranium labelled ER-1470, was half again as large as "Zinj" and no where near so heavily buttressed and flanged, but it was of roughly the same date. Clearly the transition that was to produce the Pithecanthropines from the Australopithecines was half accomplished. The face was still large and of Australopithecine form, but the braincase was definitely modified in a Pithecanthropine direction. It

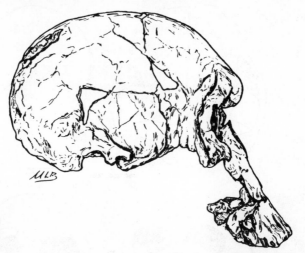

KNM ER-1470, a transitional Australopithe-cine/Pithecanthropine skull from east of Lake Turkana. Drawn from a cast.

is specimens such as this that show how arbitrary it is to divide an evolutionary continuum into pat stages, however useful they may be in general.

But if one group of Australopithecines evolved into Pithecanthropines, another group clearly did not. Both forms are now shown to be contemporaries in the East Turkana area being worked by Richard Leakey and his associates. The skull ER-406, found at Ileret in 1969, is an obvious robust Australopithecine (brain size = 510 cc.), and yet it is a contemporary of the 1.3 million year old ER-3733 skull found at Koobi Fora in 1975 (also in the East Turkana area) which is an unmistakable Pithecanthropine (brain size = 800 — 900 cc.). It was the discovery of ER-3733 that really provided the clincher to the view that some form of *Homo* lived at the same time as some form of *Australopithecus*, and one could argue that this is as close to the real "wolf" as we are likely to come.

If the continuing work of the Leakey family during the last few years has given us the pieces with which we can provide a rationale for how the Australopithecines ended and the Pithecanthropines began, the same years have produced evidence that helps us understand something of how the Australopithecines began. Starting in 1972, a series of field seasons by a French-American group has worked the Pliocene deposits in the badlands of the Afar depression north of Addis Ababa in northern Ethiopia.

Conditions for pursuing research were considerably less than promising. The climate is harsh in the extreme—an unrelieved, blazing desert heat. And however unprepossessing it may seem, the area has been politically contended for years, with intermittent sniping, raiding, and armed forays. But the Pliocene strata lie flat and workable, filled with fossil bones, and datable by the K/Ar technique. So with ingenuity, persistence, and courage, the French geologist Maurice Taieb and the American anthropologist Donald C. Johanson led crews on yearly efforts until full scale civil war drove them out in 1977. Their fieldwork was crowned with abundant success, their most spectacular discovery being that of a nearly complete Australopithecine skeleton late in 1974. This they christened Lucy, a tiny, indubitably female Australopithecine, barely three and a half feet tall. Although Lucy was a well-adapted biped, her arms were long in proportion to her legs. And her jaws and teeth, like those of other specimens found there, display a series

35

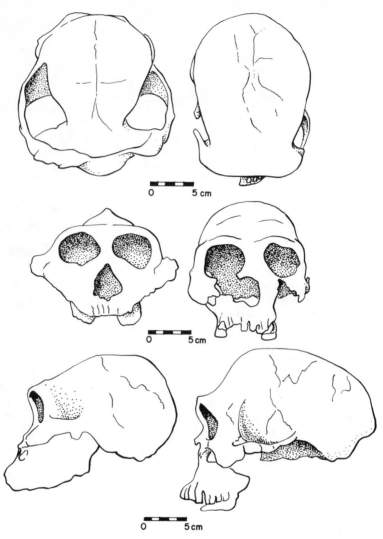

ER-406, a robust Australopithecine, and ER-3733, a Pithecan-thropine, both contemporaries in the East Turkana area of Kenya about 1.3 million years ago.

of features that are intermediate between an ape-like and a human condition. With a date of 3 million years, Lucy and her companions represent the earliest Australopithecines so far discovered. Given that degree of antiquity, a mixture of human, ape-like, and transitional features is just what we would expect to find.

But we have spent enough time recounting what was found when, and by whom, and it is time now to get on to an assessment of what it all means.

36

PART TWO *Interpreting the Evidence*

Seven Evolutionary Principles

Many approaches to the subject of human evolution are restricted to descriptions of the fossil evidence, or perhaps to the events surrounding the discovery of the major fragments. However fascinating these may be (here I suspect my own enthusiasm for the bony details of long defunct hominids may somewhat outrun that of the beginning student or general reader), they do not automatically ensure the full understanding of what is being described. Somewhere along the line, one should encounter a resume of the major principles of evolution in general, and the forces which act on humans in particular. Finally, these should be specifically applied to the human fossil record, and the role which they have played in the production of the specific noted changes should be delineated. This last will be the subject of the final chapters; meanwhile, a brief consideration will be given to the major evolutionary principles which are important to consider in human evolution.

Types Versus Populations

The study of human evolution starts with the discovery of the fossil evidence. This is then arranged in temporal sequence, and the patterns that can be discovered are interpreted according to standard evolutionary principles. Although nearly all of the current treatments discuss both evolutionary principles and the fossil evidence, one often gets the impression that the actual interpretations are being guided by unrecognized or at least unstated sets of assumptions. To the average biologist trained in the Darwinian tradition, the student of human evolution often appears to be marching to the beat of a different drummer.

We have seen how the lingering tradition of catastrophism has continued to be influential, but there are some other and equally important vestiges of traditional western world views that have continued to survive. One of these is our notion of the "typical" or "ideal." Renaissance artists portrayed human form according to what they felt were ideal proportions, and post-Renaissance biologists stocked their museums with what they hoped were typical representatives of the plants and animals of the world. In Platonic philosophy, the essence of reality was a perfect idea that was reflected in the less than perfect forms visible in the material world.

Dating from the time of St. Augustine in the fourth century A.D., currents of Platonic thought, really Neoplatonism, were combined with Christian faith to shape the way people thought about things. In this amalgamated intellectual tradition, the essence of reality, as it had been to Plato, was a perfect idea, but in this case it was an Idea in the Mind of God. Visible form can approach but it cannot attain that perfection, for to do so would be to unite it with divinity itself.

As the Renaissance age of exploration and discovery revealed to Europeans the enormous variety of plants and animals that they assumed reflected the manifold ideas in the mind of God, it became a kind of act of piety to list and describe them. To a considerable extent, this provided the impetus for the systematic pursuit of science. Whether it was Kepler working out the laws of planetary motion or Linnaeus identifying the plants and animals of the world, scientists believed they were discovering the dimensions of the mind of God and thereby coming to understand God's plan for the way things ought to be.

Since all of these categories were thought to derive from a perfect and eternal and therefore changeless Deity, the assumption followed that these ideal categories were fixed, perfect and eternal by consequence. The ideas of ash tree and aster, lobster and lion, man, mouse, and all the rest had a reality that not only derived from but proved the existence of God. To suggest that such might not be the case was tantamount to atheism or blasphemy or worse. Obviously when Darwin developed his demonstration that the only constant was change itself, operating in response to the interplay of the mechanics of impersonal natural forces, he was perceived by the pious traditionalists as an enemy to the assumed perfection and fixity of their revealed religion.

Not only did Darwin's focus on change cast doubt on the validity of fixed and changeless types, but he identified the source of that potential change in the naturally occurring variation visible among the individuals of any given species. Individual differences, then, were not just imperfect renderings of an intended ideal type. Instead they provided a vital demonstration of how a species can adapt to changing circumstances.

As a result of Darwin's insights, evolutionary biologists now realize that it is at least as important to know the naturally occurring range of variation of a given group as it is to know its idealized average. Consequently, the typological thinking of pre-Darwinian science has tended to be replaced by the populational approach of modern biology.

Old habits die hard, however, and, although it is often denounced in theory and unrecognized in fact, typological thinking is alive and well and continuing to flourish in the last quarter of the twentieth century. To an extent it is unavoidable in practice. Just to talk about things we have to give them names. And because of the nature of the fossil record, single specimens, often quite incomplete, have to do duty for whole populations and long periods of time. Scholars gain recognition for key discoveries, and inevitably the names and descriptions they give acquire an importance that smacks of typological essence with overtones of sanctity.

Finally, as was noted in the chapter on hominid catastrophism, the field of human paleontology has strong roots in the scholarship of France late in the nineteenth and early in the twentieth century. The French not only rejected a Darwinian view of evolution with its emphasis on populational thinking, but stressed a kind of Platonic essentialism. The focus on the intricacies and nuances of form in specific specimens derives from a tacit assumption that detailed description can reveal a kind of teleological intent. Inevitably, a fair portion of the typological approach survives in practice in modern anthropology, although it is generally rejected in theory.

Natural Selection

The first and most important of the evolutionary principles is encompassed by the term natural selection. Like many other basic principles in other areas of thought (culture for the anthropologist, or entropy for the physicist, for example), it is hard to define concisely, although natural scientists are virtually unanimous in its usage. Realizing that this is an oversimplification, one can regard natural selection as being the sum total of naturally occurring forces which influence the relative chances for survival and perpetuation of the various manifestations of organic life.

Credit can be given to Charles Darwin for using this as the major explanatory principle necessary to account for the cumulative change apparent in the history of any given organic line. Occasionally the principle has been tersely expressed as "survival of the fittest," although Darwin himself never stated it in these terms, and indeed they have been justly criticized as being not quite accurate. In the recent past it has been pointed out that evolutionary survival is determined more by reproductive success than by physical strength. The suggestion has been made that the phrase might be modified to read "the survival of the fit." Actually, there is a certain amount of verbal quibbling which must inevitably surround any attempt to produce a precise definition since, if fitness is described in terms of the production of viable offspring, then the fittest will obviously be those who produce the most and whose traits will be most frequently represented in subsequent generations.

As environmental forces change over time, the characteristics which have greatest survival value will not be those which were most valuable at an earlier age. However, in order that environmental forces may effect a change in the characteristic appearance of the species in question—i.e., in order for natural selection to produce evolution—some source for the new traits must be postulated. In Darwin's day this source was unknown. On the basis of extensive observational experience, however, he knew that the variants were always being produced—so he simply accepted their existence "on faith," without knowing where they came from. Some of the most bitter attacks against him came from those who recognized that he did take it that way.

Today we recognize that the faith Darwin had in his observation that variation occurs in the normal course of events was faith well-grounded. When developments in the field of genetics led to the recognition of mutations as the source of variation, it was soon explicitly realized that "mutations provide the raw materials for natural selection." As has been mentioned, this was the point where evolutionary thought and genetics joined to produce what has come to be called the synthetic theory of evolution.

The Probable Mutation Effect

If the summed forces of nature working on organic variability can be regarded as the most important principle in the production of evolutionary change, then the next most important dimension must be that which is determined by the nature and frequency of the sources of variation themselves. Simply stated, the nature of mutations, their frequency of occurrence, and the probable effect which they have are of an importance second only to natural selection.

Although a discussion of genetics at the molecular level may seem rather a long way from the human fossil record, its importance will become quite clear during the discussion of all but one of the major changes which characterize the course of human evolution. In essence, the story goes like this: During the last twenty-five years, research has identified the basic genetic material, postulated its structure, and suggested the mode of action whereby it controls organic form and function, as well as replicates itself. To say that the basic genetic material is DNA is true enough, but to say that a mutation is an error in the attempt by a DNA molecule to copy itself, while true, is not precise enough for our purposes. To appreciate the significance of the average mutation, one must first have some idea of how genetic control normally works.

For the moment we are concerned with two kinds of organic molecules: nucleic acids and proteins. Both are polymers—that is, they are chain-like structures whose links are called amino acids in the case of proteins and nucleotides in the case of nucleic acids. The full nucleic acid molecule is a double chain composed of identical halves, each being the complement or mirror image of the other. However, whereas the double chain of a nucleic acid is built up of only four different kinds of nucleotides in all possible combinations, there are more than 20 kinds of amino acids available for the construction of a protein.

Both kinds of molecules are of vital importance. Proteins not only form the structural building-blocks of which living organisms are constructed (bone, muscle, fiber), but they also constitute the organic catalysts called enzymes, hormones, and other such enabling molecules as hemoglobin, insulin, and adrenalin, without which normal metabolic functioning and growth could not occur. DNA, on the other hand, remains within the nucleus of the cell, where it provides a source of information for the construction of protein molecules.

At first it was not known how the four nucleotides of nucleic acids related to the 20-plus amino acids of proteins. To simplify the rather complex process that subsequent research has shown is involved, let us put it this way: Various sequences of nucleotides, taken three at a time, can specify (serve as a code for) given amino acids. The nucleotides, with the aid of specific enzymes, fasten together the amino acids by means of a phosphate energy bond. In the course of protein production, quantities of nucleotide triplets attach themselves to free amino acids and tow them to the sites of protein synthesis within the cell, where they are lined up and snapped together.

This brief and actually grossly oversimplified description is not intended to be complete. The point to be made is that a sequence of three specific nucleotides identifies one particular amino acid. If by chance an error is made in the replication of the nucleic acid molecule, the smallest identifiable change will be the modification of a single nucleotide. Although a single nucleotide does not correspond to an entire amino acid, the modification of any one nucleotide will indeed change the nature of the triplet to which it belongs, and in all likelihood this in turn will code a different amino acid from the previous one—if indeed it codes any.

Two of the most likely changes at the single nucleotide level result in still further complications. The addition or deletion of a nucleotide will not only modify the triplet within which it occurs, but will also change the nature of the triplets that follow. Obviously, this means more than one amino acid in the related protein will be changed, and it seems quite clear that the protein will not work in the way it was intended. A change in even one amino acid can drastically alter the function of the protein of which it is a part, as can be seen in sickle cell anemia and a variety of other deficiency diseases of an inherited nature.

What we have been discussing forms the basis for the fact realized half a century ago that the great majority of mutations will be disadvantageous to the organism in which they occur. Actually this statement, while correct, assumes a static picture in which environmental forces remain unchanged— that is, it assumes that any modification in an organism will be detrimental to it. To be sure, when an organism is well adapted to its environment, most alterations in its form which arise by chance will not be advantageous, but

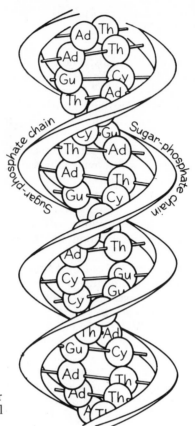

The double helix, or
Watson-Crick, model
of a DNA molecule.

there is always the case to be considered where the environment itself undergoes a change, in which instance there may be some structures which will be less important for the organism's survival. While this is not a major problem in evolution, it is one which continually arises, and, since it has apparently occurred in the course of human development, it deserves some attention.

When some major change occurs in a creature's environment, or when it enters an entirely new one, it may suddenly find that it possesses some structures which, while not disadvantageous, are of no particular value to it. Since the structures in question are neither selected for nor selected against, they are at the mercy of random variation. It is now pertinent to ask what sort of variations are likely to occur. If we are dealing with a feature of gross morphology (teeth, horns, pigmentation), we must realize that these are the products of a period of growth during which development is influenced by the sequential interaction of a sizable series of enzymes. Since enzymes are protein molecules, evidently many of them will be subject to direct genetic control, with mutations affecting their amino acid constituents.

Random variation in a morphological feature usually occurs in modifications of this growth process, and the commonest modification of the growth process is in the form of mutations affecting the controlling enzymes. At this level, the expected change is the alteration of a single amino acid, and almost invariably the result is either that the enzyme fails to work altogether, or

44

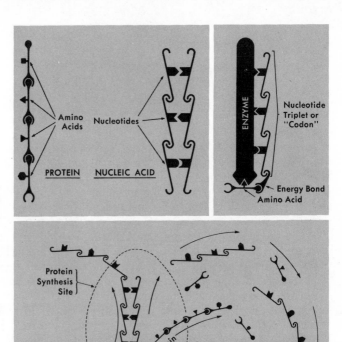

Schematic representation of a protein molecule, made up of amino acid units in a chain; and of a nucleic acid molecule, made up of nucleotide units in a chain. Right, attachment of a specific amino acid to a particular nucleotide triplet with the aid of an enzyme specially constructed for that purpose. Bottom, amino acids being towed by nucleotide triplets to the site where they are hooked together to form proteins.

that it does not work as well as it did in its unaltered form. If a growth enzyme fails to work, or works only to a reduced degree, then the structure which depends upon it either will fail to occur, or else will occur in reduced or only partially developed form. Stated briefly, the most likely effect of the most likely mutation will be the reduction of a structure which depends upon it; i.e., the result of the probable mutation effect is structural reduction. In a normally adapted organism, such reductions will of course be disadvantageous; on the other hand, wherever circumstances are altered so that a structure no longer has the same importance for survival that it previously had, one can predict that the probable mutation effect will produce its ultimate reduction.

Genetic Drift

If the importance of the probable mutation effect is minor in comparison with that of natural selection, then the importance of genetic drift is practically negligible. Basically, it is the operation of chance as it influences the distribution of characteristics in a sequence of generations. This can easily be demonstrated by a simple example. Imagine a small, isolated band of Palaeolithic hunters—say, six men and six women—encamped in a rock shelter at

Normal ....the ten hen net

Mutated by
deletion of H ......tet⌐(h) enh enn et

or,
addition of T......tth(t) ete nhe nne t

or,
substitution
of N for H.........tne(n) ten(h) hen net

The effects of deletion, addition, and substitution on the "sense" of a phrase made up of three-letter words (triplets) composed of only four kinds of letters (nucleotides). For purposes of illustration, alterations are made in the second position only, although in fact they could occur anywhere.

the edge of a game-filled valley. Hunting is good, and since they are the only people in that part of the world, their future seems well assured. A noticeable peculiarity among the men is that, whereas four of them have a full head of hair (as did their fathers, even in advancing age), the other two, having inherited the tendency to become prematurely bald, sport at best only thinning patches of what once were long, healthy locks. On one unfortunate day the roof of their rock shelter caves in, crushing most of the band of hunters—several of the women, and all but two of the men. As luck would have it, both of the unscathed men are the balding ones. On the strength of this characteristic alone, one could safely predict that the future males of the band would tend to be bald as well. (Actually, this little example portrays a particular form of genetic drift called the founder effect—but it will nevertheless suffice to illustrate the logic of the general principle.)

Evidently it was sheer chance which affected the future of the male contingent of our little group. Sheer chance is a much more important element in determining proportions where a small group is concerned than with a large group. In a population of several thousand, for instance, the accidental loss of four men will not appreciably affect the relative proportions of characteristics transmitted to future generations, as it did in our example. Chance occurrences of this or any other sort cannot impart any consistent direction to evolution or account for an evolutionary trend. Since all major evolutionary developments are the result of forces which operate over very long periods of time, genetic drift is clearly of only local or incidental importance.

There are two reasons for mentioning genetic drift. First, it has been frequently invoked (too frequently, in fact) to account for changes which appear to have no adaptive significance. Second, throughout much of prehistory the characteristic human breeding population was just the sort of small, semi-isolated group in which genetic drift could have its greatest effect. While it is difficult to point with certainty to human features which owe their existence to the operation of genetic drift, it would be equally foolish to deny that this had played any role in human evolution.

Orthogenesis

Although orthogenesis is not really an evolutionary principle at all, it has been a prominent feature of former evolutionary schemes. It is considered

46

here only so that it can be convincingly renounced. In the past, when evolutionary principles were dimly understood and did not seem adequate to account for the developments which the fossil record and contemporary organic diversity revealed, it seemed to some scholars that the visible evolutionary trends could be explained only by invoking mystical principles of unknown or supernatural guidance. Whether the forces invoked were cited as being "vital principles" or simply "evolutionary momentum," the result was the continuation of evolutionary development in a given direction for no obvious or logical reason. Straight-line development of this kind is what "orthogenesis" means.

There is no reason why development cannot occur in a consistent direction, provided that the selective forces which produce it continue to operate over long periods of time—and, clearly, this has happened in the evolutionary record. The main objections which the modern synthetic theory of evolution has to orthogenesis are its inherent implications that there is an unknowable force involved, and that development, once started in a particular direction, will continue of its own momentum even after its initial stimulus has ceased to operate. As is now realized, evolution is completely opportunistic. It is simply the accumulation of organic responses to continuing environmental stimuli. When these stimuli cease, the responses cease as well. In this sense, then, we must deny that orthogenesis is a valid evolutionary phenomenon.

Neoteny

Some aspects of human form recall the infantile. In all newborn mammals the head is relatively large and the face is relatively small in comparison with their proportions when adulthood is finally reached. In the human adult, however, the head is still noticeably large and the face relatively underdeveloped if the standards of comparison are typical mammals such as horses, dogs, rats or sheep. An adult that displays the features of infancy is said to exhibit *neoteny*, literally "the retention of the new."

The newborn human is remarkably helpless by most mammalian standards, and the period of juvenile dependence is noticeably prolonged. It is during this long immature period of play and trial-and-error behavior that the growing human learns about the world. Human beings have carried a dependence upon learned behavior to the maximum, and, conversely, almost everything that could be considered instinctive behavior has been eliminated. If this is a slower way of producing an adult that can cope with its world, it also results in an adult that can handle the new and different in much more effective fashion. In human beings, the teachability of youth is extended throughout the rest of life.

Some scholars have tried to view these various human capacities and features as simple manifestations of neoteny, a biological rendering of the poet Wordsworth's vision of the child as father of the man. The reliance on such imagery, however, encourages a tendency to confuse processes that are best treated separately. The adaptive advantage in the emphasis on braininess is obvious. The small human face—that is, small by prehuman or even Middle

Pleistocene human standards—is not simply the product of retention of a supposedly advantageous juvenile condition, but rather the result of a failure to grow. Face development and brain development are under the control of completely separate sets of selective forces and the proportion observed in comparing their relative development has no adaptive significance in itself. To invoke neoteny to account for that proportion, then, in fact explains nothing at all. Then when one looks at the rest of the human body, it is obvious that the elongated legs and relatively short trunk of the human adult are actually the reverse of being neotenous. The application of the concept of neoteny to the human condition has tended to result in oversimplifications that have inhibited our ability to understand how modern human form has actually evolved.

Sexual Dimorphism

Sensitivity to the normal range of variation is important to the student of evolution, but sometimes the unstated referent can inhibit a proper appreciation of what that normal range might be. For example, when we try to project a reconstruction of the range of variation of a fossil human population from a few scrappy specimens, we tend to do so with the model of the normal modern range in mind. To be sure, this is better than the approach that stresses the identification of an invariant typological ideal, but it does make the assumption that the nature of human variation in the past was the same as it is in the present. That in itself is a kind of teleological assumption, and it has created more than a little misunderstanding.

Obviously variation was just as normal prehistorically as it is now, but that does not mean that the *nature* of variation was the same. In fact, there is considerable evidence to suggest that it was not. This can be appreciated by a quick consideration of crucial differences in life way between moderns and the people of remote antiquity.

In the postindustrial world, there are very few jobs that cannot be done equally well by males and females. Men are just as good at cooking and changing diapers as women are at driving bulldozers and laying bricks. Only in the physical acts of procreation and the mechanics of bearing offspring are there any evolutionary forces continuing to maintain the differences in the male and female physiques.

This, however, was not true in the past. Before bottles and synthetic nipples were invented, a nursing mother was the sole source of nourishment for the infants upon whom the future of a population had to depend. In order to assure population continuity, the average human female spent her entire adult career either pregnant or lactating. Inevitably, the burdens of group defense fell upon the males. Also inevitably, the unencumbered mobility necessary for systematic, large-animal hunting restricted such activities to males. The different requirements of male and female roles led to the development of those secondary sexual distinctions in size, shape and muscularity that are still visible if no longer necessary for survival.

And if one projects this kind of expectation back into the Pleistocene and beyond—to even simpler levels of technology, one should expect to find greater degrees of male-female distinction. At the very earliest stage of hominid development where tools were rudimentary, the role of group defense must have led to the development of a degree of size and muscularity differences between males and females that attained an order of magnitude not visible in the present or the recent past.

Among the terrestrial non-human primates—for example, baboons and gorillas—the selective pressure differences acting on the male involvement with group maintenance and group defense as opposed to those acting on the female involvement with pregnancy and infant nurture have ensured the development of a marked degree of male-female difference or sexual dimorphism. In both gorillas and baboons, males are literally double the size of females. Since defensive tools are entirely lacking, selection has stressed the development of enlarged canine teeth—again especially in the males.

With this kind of perspective shaping our expectations, we ought to be alert to the possibility that sexual dimorphism among the earliest hominids was maintained to an extent that was quite beyond what a study of the modern human range of variation would lead us to anticipate. Since they did wield crude tools as defensive weapons rather than employing canine teeth, we would not expect to find a gorilloid degree of male-female canine dimorphism, but we should not be surprised if there in fact had been a gorilloid degree of dimorphism in size and muscularity.

This in turn leads to a final matter that deserves some mention. If males and females differ to such a marked degree, then obviously any attempt to represent the group by a detailed description of only one specimen is going to constitute serious misrepresentation. In fact, it is just possible that some of the descriptions of different genera or species in the literature may be depictions of males and females of a single group. These points will all be kept in mind when we turn our attention to the actual fossil evidence for the stages of human evolution.

Humanity's Adaptation

Before embarking upon the final synthesis, wherein the foregoing insights are applied to the interpretation of the course of human evolution, we should give some attention to the age-old question, "What is man?" Definitions range from the realm of morality and philosophy to the pragmatic, functional, and physical. Depending on one's viewpoint, the more philosophical definitions can be characterized as displaying either dimensions of soaring insight or miasmas of vague verbalization. In any case, this realm will be left to other scholars with other purposes.

Attempts have been made to define humanity by means of specific, measurable, anatomical criteria, with the implication that such definitions are somehow "objective." In the eighteenth century, an eminent Dutch naturalist distinguished the human condition as indicated by the lack of an intermaxillary bone, and only within the last few years, anatomists have tried to claim that a brain capacity of at least 750 cc. is the minimum human criterion. The trouble with such criteria is that inevitable exceptions can be found, and that ultimately there is no necessary relation between them and the condition of being human. Definitions are created by people for their own convenience; although of great use, they are nevertheless arbitrary and subjective.

Viewed in evolutionary perspective, the most fruitful definition of humanity should be that which touches upon its most distinctive adaptation. Whereas arguments can be produced favoring the human brain in this regard, the social scientist can quickly counter this by pointing out that man does not survive by brain alone; however valuable it may be, brain does not serve as a substitute for experience. The most characteristic part of being human is the ability to profit from the accumulated and transmitted experience of other human beings. This can be regarded as man's most important adaptation, and it is what the anthropologist means by the term culture.

It is important to realize that culture, the primary human adaptive mechanism, is not a facet of human anatomy; in fact, some have referred to it as an "extra-somatic adaptation." Evidently, any attempt to define humanity on the basis of anatomy alone will be doomed to failure. This is not to say that human anatomy is unrelated to culture; as we shall see, quite the reverse is the case. But the anatomical correlates to the fact of cultural existence are reflections of an already existing dimension, and must be regarded as being after the fact rather than of primary importance in and of themselves.

This ability to transmit information and experience from one individual to another and from one generation to another is most clearly recognizable in languages, and the records of their use. Unfortunately, however diagnostic language may be as an indicator of humanity, it leaves no trace in the archaeological or fossil record prior to the invention of writing—and, since the vast majority of the happenings in human evolution occurred prior to this event, this puts the prehistorian in the somewhat awkward position of trying to evaluate the humanity of our finds in the absence of the best criterion. Inevitably, the only tangible evidence for prehistoric human cultural capacity is prehistoric tools. This narrowing of the focus has even led some archaeologists to claim that the manufacture of tools should itself be the ultimate criterion of humanity, defining people as tool-making animals. One consequence of this has been a heightened concern for tool use, as opposed to tool manufacture, due to the feeling that a creature which merely selected suitably shaped natural objects as tools does not deserve to be called fully human. On the other hand, a creature which engaged in the regular modification of raw materials according to a set pattern could be appropriately elevated to the realm of the human. Contributing towards this appraisal was the fact that prehistoric stone tools can be traced back to the point where the amount of shape modification is so rudimentary that they are little more than selected hunks of rock. Some archaeologists have felt that at this point we reach the boundary between the human and the prehuman.

There are several reasons why this latter assumption should be greeted with scepticism. First, field observation shows that modern chimpanzees engage in a little simple tool manufacture. Next, merely because the prehistoric creature in question was perhaps not shaping stone does not necessarily mean that he was not shaping perishable materials which are manifestly easier to modify. Finally, the dichotomy between the simple selection of appropriately shaped raw materials and tool manufacture artificially creates categories out of what should be a whole zone of transition and which is unrelated to the question of whether or not the survival of the user depended upon the accumulated and transmitted experience of previous generations.

Properly speaking, the mere presence of shaped or unshaped tools in the archaeological record is of symbolic value. To the prehistorian they symbolize the fact that the user was utilizing a dimension of patterned behavior of an order of complexity which is too great to have been discovered anew each generation. Such behavior could be acquired only by enculturation—the process of growing up in a social environment conditioned by the accumulated and transmitted learning of previous generations. Given no more than this, we must recognize that, however rudimentary, the verbal clues, which undoubtedly assisted both the enculturation process and the activities which the presence of the tools symbolize, constituted a simple form of language. Furthermore, although our knowledge of the exact use to which these early tools were put is rather limited, it is quite apparent that they were vital to the survival of the users.

With nothing more than the existence of stone tools, then, we can infer a creature which possessed culture in the anthropological sense, and which could not have survived without it. By our definition, such a creature deserves the designation "human being."

Eight Cultu
as an Ecological Nich

With the presence of stone tools considered as sufficient to establish the existence of a culture-dependent creature—a genuine hominid—then one must recognize the fact that some form of human being must have been in existence in the early Pleistocene, some two million years ago. The Pleistocene is the name for the geological period which contained the recently ended ice age. Since this was the period during which all of the major events of human evolution have taken place, it has necessarily been the focus of considerable attention on the part of the anthropological world.

Recently, geophysicists have utilized a variety of ingenious techniques to establish the age of strata in the recent past. Recognizing that various radioactive elements "decay" into stable end products at fixed rates, they have measured, in material taken from crucial geological layers, the ratio of certain of these radioactive elements to their end products. Since the ratio discovered is proportional to the length of time during which the process has been going on, this serves as a measure of the time elapsed since the layer in question was formed. By these means, the Pleistocene has been calculated to extend from about two million down to some 10,000 years ago.

Perhaps we have made Pleistocene dating seem simpler than it is. Actually, there are a great many knotty problems connected with it. For instance, finding suitable mineral specimens to use for this kind of analysis is beset with difficulties. Indeed, only a very limited number of layers have been pinned down in this way; the rest have been tentatively fitted in by extrapolations based on the fossil animals contained. As a result, a great deal of uncertainty still remains concerning such problems as the correlations and relative ages of layers in South Africa with those in Indonesia, or Europe with China. Despite all these uncertainties and inaccuracies, however, the temporal dimensions of the period during which humanity evolved are beginning to emerge.

During the Pleistocene there were four major onsets of glacial conditions in the Northern Hemisphere. Geologists used to regard this period as being entirely taken up by the glaciations and the milder intervening periods called interglacials, but recently the beginning of the Pleistocene has been extended back to include a long, mild stretch called the Villafranchian. The divisions of the Pleistocene and their approximate time durations are displayed in the chart.

DATE (years ago)	PLEISTOCENE DIVISIONS	GLACIAL STAGE	CULTURAL STAGE
10,000	Recent	Post (?) Glacial	Atomic Age / Neolithic
	Upper Pleistocene	Würm	Upper Palaeolithic
30,000			Middle Palaeolithic
100,000		3rd Interglacial	(Mousterian)
	Middle Pleistocene	Riss	Lower Palaeolithic.
			(Acheulian)
		2nd Interglacial	
		Mindel	(Abbevillian)
500,000		1st Interglacial	
	Lower Pleistocene	Günz	
	Villafranchian	Pre-Günz?	
1.75 million			(Oldowan)
4 million?			

The divisions of the Pleistocene showing the four major glacial stages with corresponding dates and cultural developments. Recently, evidence has been produced to show that a four- or even five-stage scheme may be much too simple. Note also that the time scale becomes increasingly compressed toward the early end.

The most consistent and reliable evidence for human existence throughout this time is to be seen in the form of chipped stone artifacts. The tool-making traditions practiced during the Pleistocene have been given the label Palaeolithic (old stone), and reveal the fact that the characteristic modes of subsistence were hunting and gathering. The change to a food-producing way of life did not begin to occur until after the Pleistocene was over. (Although this change surely was one of the most significant cultural events that ever occurred, treatment of it will be deferred until after the stages of human evolution have been considered.)

The Palaeolithic is further divisible into Upper, Middle (tentatively), and Lower segments of very unequal length. Ninety to 95 percent of the human span was spent in the Lower Palaeolithic, during which cultural change was extremely slow and cultural diversity apparently at a minimum. One says "apparently," since all we know of the Lower Palaeolithic is the few stone tools remaining and the bones of the animals which people ate. While these indicate that the gross dimensions of human life were much the same from one end of the inhabited world to the other, it is perfectly possible and even likely that minor cultural differences of an unknown nature flourished in different areas. Stone tools form only a small component of the total cultural repertoire, which one should remember includes far greater quantities of perishable items and, even more important, dimensions of language, knowledge, and social behavior which leave no record. Potential diversity of this sort notwithstanding, however, it is still possible to state that major and basic facets of human adaptation were substantially the same from one end of the Old World to the other. Whether in South Africa, Europe, or Indonesia, game was hunted by the same techniques and processed by chipped stone tools which were virtually identical over vast areas.

The increasing local diversity visible in the stone tools of the Middle and Upper Palaeolithic will be treated later, but at the moment our concern is with the Lower Palaeolithic, and specifically with its earliest phases. According to current indications, the oldest cultural remains in the world, and consequently the earliest evidence for human existence, come from East and South Africa. The tools on which this judgment is based are of the crudest recognizable sort, and, were it not for the location in which they have been found, it would be almost impossible to prove that they were indeed the products of deliberate manufacture. But, occurring as they do by ancient lake margins and out on the plains miles from the nearest potential rock outcrop or natural source, one can only conclude that they were deliberately transported there. The discovery of such objects in a rocky stream bed or a wave-cut shore would excite no interest at all, for they are indistinguishable from the countless thousands of pebbles and cobbles which natural water action has battered and fractured. But found in a fine sedimentary deposit amidst the dismembered remains of extinct animals, they clearly indicate the activities of an ancient hunter.

In their crudest form, these early tools resemble river pebbles from which a flake or two has been knocked off, creating an edge or point. This is the source of the type designation by which they are known—"pebble tools." Because of the simple nature of the flaking, it is impossible to say whether it

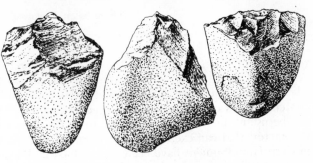

Pebble tools of the Oldowan type from Bed I of Olduvai Gorge, Tanzania. (By permission of the Trustees of the British Museum [Natural History].)

was done deliberately, or whether it had occurred naturally and the ancient hominid had simply chosen the stone from among others for this reason. The controversy over the importance of tool manufacture as distinguished from tool use has been mentioned in the preceding chapter. While this will probably never be resolved, the important thing to remember is that the presence of these tools, whether chosen or fashioned, signifies the presence of a creature whose life depended upon the behavioral complex of which these tools were a part, i.e., whose life depended upon the presence of culture.

There is another crucial fact to be realized, and that is that there is evidence for no more than one basic cultural tradition in the early Pleistocene. By tracing this up through time, it is evident that this tradition is the direct ancestor of all succeeding cultural traditions—which makes it, among other things, the remote parent of this book. A single original cultural tradition strongly suggests that only one organism developed culture as a necessary condition for its survival.

Ecology is the study of the life-ways of species, and the total life-way of a given species can be called its ecological niche. In the human case, all facets of living are conditioned by culture, and it is therefore justifiable to regard humans as inhabiting a cultural ecological niche. There is another ramification of evolutionary theory which has been called the competitive exclusion principle, and this states that no two organisms can continue to occupy the same ecological niche. In a sense, this is stating the obvious, although, as in so much else, it is not always obvious until stated. The point is this: Not only is culture a single ecological niche within which one would expect to find only a single species, but since there is only one cultural tradition visible in the early Pleistocene, the probability is greatly increased that there has been only one hominid species at any one time, and that the hominids of different time levels are lineally related.

But if culturally dependent creatures of different time levels are probably related, what about the occurrence of two different forms of hominid at the same time? How could that occur with competition within a niche—the cultural ecological niche in this case—tending to eliminate one of the competing forms? We can only guess that at its earliest stages of development, culture was less effective and consequently was a less than all-pervasive determinant of the nature of the total life-way that it eventually came to dominate. Evidently more than one creature made an effort to enter the cultural ecological niche, but, in the long run, only one continued.

The term cultural ecological niche, then, is an abstraction that we can use for our own convenience. But as biologists have found when they have tried to define other kinds of ecological niches, one must be careful lest a convenient abstraction be raised to the level of a typological essence. The concept of ecological niche is a convenient way of generalizing about organic adaptation and no more, but it should not be allowed to take on an idealized existence of its own. For making broad generalizations, such categorizations can be useful, but we must continue to be aware of the particular and separate factors that can exert very specific influences. If the general capacities of modern *Homo sapiens* have been conditioned by long-term adaptation to the cultural ecological niche, some obvious differences—skin color, nose form— are the product of regional differences in the intensity of selective forces that themselves are distributed without regard to human cultural capacities. In short, it is a useful concept, but we have to be careful that it does not turn around and use us.

Just as the evidence for cultural development can be viewed in terms of sequential stages, so can the picture of human physical development, although its stages are considerably more tentative because of the fragmentary nature of the record and the long time gaps betwen crucial specimens. For the earlier stages, the fossil evidence is spotty and widely separated, with the relative ages of the various localities bitterly contested. For most of the later stages the evidence is more complete, the dating more reliable, and the association with the cultural record more certain. In spite of this improvement, however, there are still many problems and disputed pieces of evidence, and many professional scholars are vehemently opposed to the implications of the solution about to be offered. Speculation is rife, and since no interpretation can be more than that, the best justification for the interpretation that follows is that it is consistent with both cultural and evolutionary theory.

Nine The
Australopithecine Stage

Africa, which has provided us with the earliest archaeological evidence for human existence, has also yielded the earliest hominid skeletal remains. The term "hominid" is a colloquial version of the technical term *Hominidae*, the taxonomic family to which human beings belong. The closest human relatives within the order *Primates* are the living anthropoid apes. These belong in the family *Pongidae*, which, together with the *Hominidae*, is included within the superfamily *Hominoidea*. To simplify matters of reference, the term "pongid" is generally used to designate anything which is more ape-like than man-like, while the term "hominid" is generally used to mean "taxonomically included within the family which harbors human beings proper."

The initial specimen, *Australopithecus africanus*, has given its name to a whole group of what are variously called "ape-men," "man-apes," "near-men," or even "primitive men." These include the Transvaal finds by Dart, Broom, Robinson, and others, and the category can also be extended to include "Zinj" and other specimens from Bed I at Olduvai, many of Richard Leakey's discoveries east of Lake Turkana, material from the Omo River valley in southern Ethiopia, and the Pliocene finds of more than three million years antiquity made by Johanson in the Afar depression of central Ethiopia, and at Laetolil, 25 miles south of Olduvai in Kenya, by Mary Leakey. Broom and others have attempted to elevate these to subfamilial status within family *Hominidae* and call them Australopithecinae. This would allow the retention of all the separate generic names as valid taxonomic units, but, in terms of the present analysis this course of action seems untenable. It is still useful to refer to the group as Australopithecines, and, as will be seen, they can properly be regarded as the first full stage in human evolution.

The differences of opinion concerning Australopithecine taxonomy revolve around the criteria that are considered important for purposes of classification. For Broom and Robinson, visually perceived differences and similarities are of prime importance, with taxonomic status depending on how many there are of each. Thus, the Australopithecines are ape-like in the possession of small brain cases, big molar teeth, facial projection, and a number of other features, but they differ from the apes in that they lack projecting canines, have a downward instead of a backward facing *foramen magnum* (hole at the base of the skull where the spinal chord enters), and have a shortened and expanded ilium (hip bone) and other related characteristics. In this latter regard they resemble humans more than apes, and Broom and Robinson (and others) consider that this balance of human and pongid features justifies a taxonomic position distinct from the one occupied by modern humanity, and of greater importance than merely either a specific or generic distinction. Note, however, that they can still be formally considered within family *Hominidae*, and hence they are called hominids.

Without denying that the balance of Australopithecine characteristics hangs somewhere between the pongid and hominid categories, it is worth pointing out that not all characteristics are of equal importance to the survival of the organism. It would seem that those characteristics which have the greatest adaptive significance should be the ones to determine the major taxonomic category. In the case of the Australopithecines, two characteristics outweigh all others, but it is not so much the characteristics themselves as what they signify. The first is the nonprojecting canine and the second is the fact that the Australopithecines were erect walking bipeds. Although these features have been recognized for years—in fact, they have largely contributed

Artist's conception of an Australopithecine. Note the simple look on his face and the long, ape-like arms. This is sheer fancy since there is no way of telling facial expression from the fossil record, and there is no evidence that the arms were particularly long.

to the fact that the Australopithecines are generally included within the category hominid—their full significance has been only dimly perceived.

To take up the first of these, it is most suggestive that the Australopithecines and subsequent human beings, alone of all the terrestrial primates, do not have projecting canine teeth. Typically, terrestrial primates have greatly enlarged canines (witness the baboons), since, as small, relatively slow creatures, they could not survive the depredations of a variety of carnivores without some effective means of defense. The lack of an anatomical means of defense in humans is obviously compensated for by possession of a manufactured weaponry, and it is difficult to interpret the Australopithecines in any other light.

The other point to consider is the fact that the Australopithecines were bipeds, as can be seen from the anatomy of the pelvis and leg, and the placement of the skull. Admittedly it was fashionable in a generation gone by to envision the Palaeolithic hunter bounding across the grasslands on his long, straight legs, as though bipedalism were somehow the most efficient and "best" possible way of getting around. To any who may still harbor the lingering residue of such an illusion, I suggest that you seriously consider the vision summoned up by an irate adult *Homo sapiens* in hot pursuit of a thoroughly frightened *Felis domesticus* (house cat). As a mechanism for high-speed locomotor efficiency, hominid bipedalism is ludicrous. Obviously a creature which cannot even catch a small cat has even less chance of getting away from a large one, and it is certain that such felines as leopards and lions, as well as a variety of pack-hunting canines, must have posed a constant threat to the survival of any savanna-dwelling primate during the Pleistocene.

The only possible excuse for the development of hominid bipedalism is that it allowed for the development of compensating features (but clearly not formidable canines). Since the main functional correlate of bipedalism is the fact that the hands are freed from any involvement in the locomotor process, it would seem that they must have been used in wielding a non-anatomical defensive mechanism. Given a creature lacking dental defenses and pathetically slow on foot, we could postulate the existence of culture even *without* any direct evidence. Culture, in the form of recognizable but rudimentary stone tools, does exist right back to the beginning of the Pleistocene two million years ago, and it is evidently ancestral to the subsequent traditions of the Middle and Upper Pleistocene where it is clearly the manufactured product of our own forebears. Furthermore, the hominids at that time were all recognizable as Australopithecines.

Not very many years ago, we could feel a sense of gratification in the association of the earliest demonstrable evidence for culture with hominids whose anatomy indicates that they could not have survived without it. As we have since discovered, however, things are not quite so simple. On the one hand, in the Hadar region of the Afar depression in north-central Ethiopia and at Laetolil, just south of Olduvai Gorge in Tanzania, there are abundant remains of recently discovered Australopithecines that date back more than three million years. This is well back into the Pliocene and about a million years before the first stone tools. And then shortly after stone tools put in their appearance, there is clear evidence for two distinct kinds of Australopithecine. Finally, by 1.3 million years ago, we find a more developed stone tool assemblage, Australopithecines, and full-fledged Pithecanthropines. Given these data, we can legitimately ask, "What does it all mean?" Can we interpret it in such a way that we can get some sense of what was going on? In the current vernacular, what is the "scenario" that this suggests? Admittedly, there are many pieces of information not mentioned in the above sketch that can bear on the question, but many are so scrappy and incomplete that they are just as likely to confuse as to clarify. Despite that, it is indeed possible to sketch the outlines of a synthesis.

The Origin of Hunting

One of the keys to our understanding is the realization of what the evidence does and what it does not tell us concerning the dimensions of the cultural ecological niche. As we have noted, the presence of manufactured tools is direct evidence for the existence of culture, and this in turn has led us to anticipate the presence of those other aspects we have come to associate with it—expanded dependence on learning, symbolic behavior, planning for the future, and the like. These are inferences, however, and the presence of tools *per se* provides no more evidence in their support than does the existence of a biped that does not have projecting canine teeth.

On the other hand, the context and associations of the tools can tell us more than the not-so-insignificant fact that their makers depended on culture for survival. The shape of the worked stone pieces themselves is not particularly instructive: The early ones are about the size of a dinner roll with a flake or two knocked off to make a pointed or chisel-like business edge. And although no one doubts that the object in making the tool had been to produce a working edge that could be employed for some important function, there has been much less certainty about what that function actually was. Guesses concerning their use have ranged from suggestions that they were employed for digging roots, for shaping wooden objects, or as hand-held weapons; and artists' reconstructions variously depict Australopithecines facing marauding carnivores or even each other with pebble tools clutched in hand in dagger-like fashion, or sprinting across the African savanna in pursuit of an antelope or gazelle while wielding their tools in a threatening manner.

One of the problems in dealing with the events of prehistory is that we can never go back and put our interpretations to any real kind of test. Instead, we have to rely on circumstantial evidence. Our conclusions, then, are tentative at best and we can only offer them with varying degrees of probability instead of proof. With perseverance, awareness, and luck, we can identify some of the situations where prehistoric activities took place. In most instances, the tools were lost or abandoned in areas unrelated to their use and then subject to repositioning by the weathering actions that generally reshape the landscape.

But in rare and fortunate cases, they remain concentrated at the scene of their actual employment with their relationships relatively undisturbed. A number of such examples have been discovered at Olduvai Gorge and east of Lake Turkana, with perhaps the most instructive being at Koobi Fora in the East Turkana area. There, a concentration of flake tools and pebble choppers occurs in the sediments of what had once been a river delta, distributed amongst the bones of an extinct hippopotamus. The scatter and positioning of the hippo bones strongly suggests that it was butchered and eaten on the site, and furthermore that the stone tools had been used to do the butchering.

Careful geological analysis at that site and in the surrounding area has enabled us to build a picture of what things were like, not only at that time, but back to more than three million years as well, and the picture is not much different from what can be seen in much of East Africa today. Large lakes lay along the north-south fault axes of the rift valleys much as do Lakes Turkana, Manyara, Eyasi, and others today. These were surrounded by grassy savanna lands which in turn were crossed by meandering watercourses that ended in deltas and swamps at the lake margins. Riverine and gallery forests were distributed along the banks of the lakes and streams. The evidence suggests that these patches of woodland were the preferred habitats of the earliest hominids, and we can guess that the availability of fruiting trees as both sources of nourishment and refuges from the threat of predators was as important to the Australopithecines as it was to baboons, then as well as now.

The hippopotamus butchery site at Koobi Fora was in the delta of one such stream where it joined the Plio-Pleistocene ancestor of Lake Turkana (formerly Lake Rudolf). There, approximately two million years ago, a band of Australopithecines encountered a hippopotamus that had died for whatever reason and been washed downstream to get mired on its side. This then became the scene of an Australopithecine banquet. Hippopotamus hide, however, is pretty well impervious to hominid teeth and fingernails, and they evidently manufactured a quantity of crude stone tools on the spot to help them get through to the edible portion. They then feasted on the exposed half of the hippo but left the other side buried in the mud and silt, where its skeleton remained undisturbed down to the smallest toe bones until it and the scatter of stone tools were excavated by Richard Leakey's team some two million years later.

At Olduvai Gorge, the careful analysis of Mary Leakey, Richard's mother, has shown that Australopithecine tools were evidently used to butcher everything from mice on up to elephants, although the most common bones are those of antelopes and smaller mammals. Modern chimpanzees and baboons will kill and eat young gazelles, bush pigs, monkeys, and other animals when the occasion arises, but it is principally an opportunistic and relatively uncommon adjunct to their normal life-way. The Plio-Pleistocene Australopithecines, however, were evidently more systematic in their use of animals as dietary sources, but one can guess that they started from a kind of chimpanzee-like opportunism and only gradually developed the skills and capabilities that transformed them into full scale hunters and proper members of the genus *Homo*.

The archaeological sequence from Bed I to the overlying Bed II at Olduvai provides the best evidence we have for that transformation. The tools at the lower levels of Bed I are crude, and the animal bones with which they are associated are generally from small creatures. By the middle of Bed II, however, tool categories display regular differentiation and it is clear that the adults of large-sized game animals were being regularly hunted. What we can see there, apparently, is the record of the transformation of a precocious bipedal ape into a full-fledged hunting hominid.

The Earlier Origin of Tool Use

Equally clearly, then, we can see that the bipedalism and related dependence upon hand-held tools of the early Australopithecines preceded the focus on hunting behavior by at least a million years. And obviously the tools being used at the earlier stages were made of perishable materials. While we can never "know" this, we can guess that the wielding of a pointed stick was the crucial element that led to the change in selective forces that produced a tool-dependent biped in the first place. As the American anthropologist S. L. Washburn has pointed out, the addition of a simple digging stick to the behavioral repertoire of a baboon could nearly double its food-getting efficiency.

To this one could add the suggestion that the digging stick redirected is a more effective defensive weapon than even the formidable canine teeth of the average male baboon. After all, to bring canine teeth into effective use, the baboon literally has to come to grips with its adversary, and if that happens to be two hundred pounds of hungry leopard, the chances are poor that even the most powerful baboon can get away unscathed. If the leopard is fended off by a five foot length of stout, pointed stick, however, the survival chances are slightly better. And if the leopard should throw caution to the winds and charge, the butt of the stick can be planted on the ground with the point directed towards the oncoming predator, which would literally impale itself.

As a dual-purpose defensive weapon and food-getting device, the digging stick would have given the earliest hominids a good competitive edge over the baboons with whom they shared the Pliocene savannas of East Africa. It is certainly plausible to suggest that these were the circumstances that led to the shaping of the ingrained tool-dependence which is the closest thing to instinctive behavior that we possess. Along with this, we would expect the development of a mode of locomotion that freed the hands for a tool-wielding role. Indeed, the essentials of hominid bipedalism were already visible in Lucy over three million years ago at Hadar.

One could object that even wielding a stout, pointed stick, a three to three-and-a-half foot tall Australopithecine would be quickly tumbled by a bat or two from a leopard's paw. But Lucy was female, and if the males of her group were double her size and robustness, then the scenario becomes more plausible. Although there is no other skeleton at that date that is anywhere near so complete as that of Lucy, there are mandibles both at Hadar (Afar) and at Laetolil which show that sexual dimorphism was quite as marked as it is in the other terrestrial primates. Even the canines and lower first premolars show an elongation that suggests a pongid condition in their not-too-distant past.

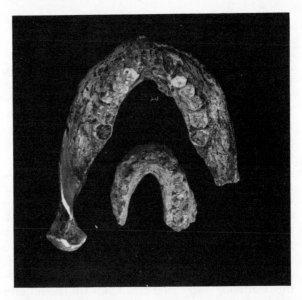

Australopithecine sexual dimorphism as illustrated by a large (SK12) and a small (SK74a) mandible from Swartkrans in the Transvaal region of South Africa. The difference in robustness greatly exceeds the greatest male–female difference one would normally encounter in a modern human population.

If the earliest Australopithecines were tool-using bipeds, there is not much reason to expect that their other adaptations were much different from those of non-human terrestrial primates. With molar teeth closer to gorilloid than chimpanzee size, they obviously depended for their nourishment on the tough seeds, nuts, roots, fruits, and vegetables that could be gleaned from the savanna and its riverine forests. The yearly round of events and their dietary elements must have been quite similar to those aspects of the life of the baboons with whom they shared the area. For that reason, we can suspect that many aspects

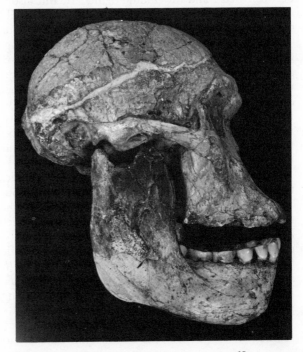

The skull of Broom's "Mrs. Ples," Sts 5, from Sterkfontein, with the jaw SK 23 from Swartkrans. Individuals from these two sites in the Transvaal of South Africa have been considered specifically or even generically distinct, but it is clear that if Mrs. Ples had not lost her teeth, she would have required a mandible of almost exactly the size represented by SK 23. The supposedly robust and gracile South African Australopithecines are very much closer in size than is commonly reported.

of their behavior may have been more like that of baboons than what we think of as characteristically human. We can guess that adult males maintained a dominance hierarchy that helped to promote group cohesion and group defense. There is no reason to suggest that there was a prolonged male-female pair bond or that sexual activity had become a year-round rather than a seasonal activity. And there is no reason to believe that they had yet lost the normal primate fur coat.

All told, the earliest hominids might strike us as more ape-like than human, despite their tools and their gait. It is this realization that has led most scholars to grant them generic distinction from true human beings. Backing off from the position I took in the first edition of this book, it seems most in line with the evidence to recognize them as belonging to genus *Australopithecus* as Dart proposed it in 1925. For the moment, there is no good reason to regard them as specifically distinct from what he described—which would make them, tentatively, *Australopithecus africanus*—always realizing that further clarifying discoveries could cast things in quite a different perspective.

Hunting and Niche Divergence

If systematic hunting was not a significant aspect of early hominid behavior for at least a million years that we know of (and possibly more that we have no evidence for as yet), it eventually became so, as the archaeological record in Olduvai Gorge shows so graphically in the cultural developments between Bed I and the middle of Bed II. But also at Olduvai and even more clearly at East Turkana, it is apparent that not all Australopithecines added a hunting component to their subsistence behavior.

The record shows butchering technology growing in sophistication through time, paralleled by increasing evidence for the successful hunting of large game animals. The record also shows that brain size was increasing and molar tooth size was reducing in one hominid line. But there is further evidence which shows that brain size did not increase in another hominid line while molar tooth size did. The Leakeys' famous "Zinj" find of 1959 has molar teeth of fully gorilloid size. Its brain is also of gorilloid size, which is to say that it is only half Pithecanthropine size and merely one-third that of the modern average.

"Zinj" at 1.75 million years is very nearly duplicated by the ER 406 skull from Ileret east of Lake Turkana half a million years more recently, by which time there is also evidence for a fully emerged Pithecanthropine— for example ER 3733 from Koobi Fora. We are constrained to accept a relationship between the evidence for increasingly successful hunting and cerebral expansion, and if that is the case, then the Australopithecines that continued on through the Lower Pleistocene *without* showing an increase in brain size were probably not engaged in systematic hunting activity. The increase in molar size to a fully gorilloid level suggests a concentration on plant food.

It would appear, then, that starting with the evidence for the first stone tools at the Plio-Pleistocene boundary, a division arose in hominid subsistence

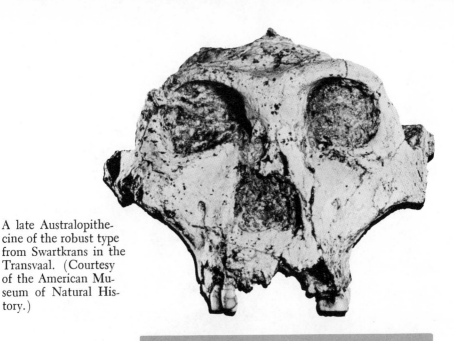

A late Australopithe-cine of the robust type from Swartkrans in the Transvaal. (Courtesy of the American Museum of Natural History.)

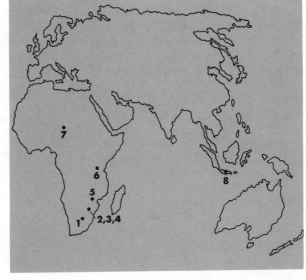

Location of Australopithecine sites: 1. Taung. 2. Sterkfontein. 3. Swartkrans. 4. Kromdraai. 5. Makapansgat. 6. Olduvai Gorge. 7. East Turkana. 8. Omo. 9. Hadar (Afar depression).

strategies between those that concentrated more on hunting and those that focussed on the products of the plant kingdom. The former became transformed into what we recognize as belonging in genus *Homo*, while the latter remained as members of genus *Australopithecus*. Since the clearest and best described example of the surviving line of robust Australopithecines was the Leakeys' *"Zinjanthropus" boisei*, and since most feel that the generic designation is unwarranted, there is a tentative feeling that the robust lineage can be identified as *Australopithecus boisei*.

At the moment we have no idea how the separation between the robust line and the lineage that evolved into *Homo* took place. Presumably some

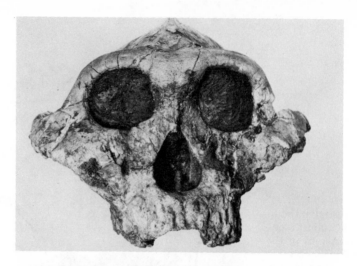

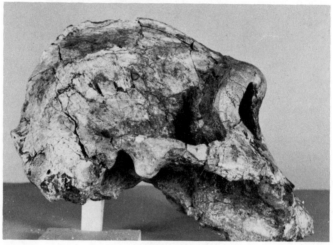

A late robust Australopithecine ER 406 above and a Pithecanthropine ER 3733 on facing page, both from the area east of Lake Turkana at about 1.3 million years ago. Note the expanded cheek bones for chewing muscle attachment in the Australopithecine, and the higher and broader braincase in the Pithecanthropine. (Courtesy of the National Museum of Kenya.)

kind of ecological event isolated one group from the other, during which time speciation occurred. This has happened often enough to have produced specific distinctions between many related groups of African monkeys, and there is no reason why it could not have occurred in the hominids at least once. Since the Australopithecines were essentially savanna dwellers, the crucial separation could have occurred during one of the damper periods when the African rain forest extended from the Congo basin all the way across East Africa to join with the east coast forest, thus separating the savanna into isolated northern and southern regions.

66

Did the northern Australopithecines develop the rudiments of hunting during that separation and take the first steps that propelled them towards becoming *Homo*? Or was it the southern group that did so? Or was it some other sequence of events? We simply have no evidence as yet. All we know is that the hunter was the only one left by the end of the Lower Pleistocene. Did they do in their vegetarian cousins? Certainly that is a possibility. And if that is a form of catastrophism, we cannot deny that such things have happened frequently enough in the fossil record. Extinctions are commoner than survivals, and it is no denial of the principles of evolution to show how the successful development of one group spells doom for another.

Ten Th

Pithecanthropine Stag

The Consequences of Hunting

The obvious skeletal changes that convert an ape into an Australopithecine are the shortening and spreading of the pelvis, accompanied by the modification of the feet for support rather than grasping, and the reduction of the formerly projecting canine teeth. These are related to the adoption of a bipedal mode of locomotion and hand-held weapons as a mode of defense. They are very ancient and fundamental developments and are united in a bio-behavioral complex that provides a necessary base for the later development of those largely behavioral traits that we have come to regard as constituting the essentials of human nature.

The obvious anatomical changes that convert an Australopithecine into a Pithecanthropine are even simpler, but the implications are at least as profound. The key element signalling that conversion is the increase in brain size. Australopithecine brain size was approximately 500 cc., which is about average for the larger of the Anthropoid apes. The Pithecanthropine average is roughly twice that, which puts it well within the lower part of the normal

68

range of variation of modern humanity. Surely this must be related to the development of that constellation of behavioral capacities that is distinctively human. Just as surely, also, it was the selective forces of the non-pongid subsistence strategy adopted by the emerging Pithecanthropines that led to that cerebral expansion and its implied behavioral correlates.

The crucial factor, as a number of observers have noted, was the adoption of a hunting life-way. In spite of the casual examples of baboon and chimpanzee predatory activity, the systematic pursuit of animals for food is a profoundly un-primate kind of activity. One could guess, then, that most of those features that make humans unique among the primates—excepting bipedalism and its correlates—are the results of the retooling that occurred when the genus *Homo* emerged as a major predator early in the Pleistocene. Since this remodelling involved only very minor visible changes from the neck on down, our focus on the importance of the brain size increase would seem to be justified.

In fact, the one postcranial change that is noticeable, if minor, appears to be more a direct correlate with brain size than with any change in bodily usage. Bipedal locomotion had been perfected during the Australopithecine stage, although there were minor ways in which the pelvis and the upper end of the femur (thigh bone) differed from modern form. Biomechanical analysis has shown that the greater iliac flare and longer femoral neck of the Australopithecines was actually more efficient than the modern condition and required less muscular effort. The modern configuration appears to have developed during the Pithecanthropine stage and it has been suggested that it was created by the development of a wider birth canal that was necessary to bear the larger-brained infants of the genus *Homo*.

Another correlate with brain size increase is a decrease in the male/female body size difference. Sexual dimorphism remained marked in the Pithecanthropines, but it had reduced from its Australopithecine extreme. The reduction in dimorphism was not caused by a decrease in male size and robustness, but rather by an increase in female size. Again, we can suspect that the selective forces that led to this were those related to the bearing of a large-brained infant. Not only that, but the business of carrying it for a full nine-month

The Pithecanthropine Stage. Note the artist's conception of early man as brutish and flea-bitten, clutching his "hand-axe."

term of pregnancy is more easily accomplished where maternal body size is larger than it had previously been.

Larger brains imply greater intellectual capabilities, and surely that was the key to the successful adoption of hunting as a subsistence strategy by early members of the genus *Homo*. But unlike brain size, intelligence is not a simple product of heredity. Realized intellectual capacity only occurs after years of trial and experience. Human intellectual achievement is vastly greater than that possible for even the brightest of our pongid relatives, but its mature form is made possible only by a prolonged period of infant and juvenile dependence during which the young are nurtured, protected, and given the benefits of the experience previously acquired by their elders. This period of prolonged dependence is only made possible by an equally long period of parental responsibility. And in a situation where hunting activities take males away from the group for days at a time, the role of instructor and protector is better played by females who are considerably larger than the three-and-a-half foot stature of the early Australopithecine females.

Although sexual dimorphism was therefore less pronounced than it had been during the Australopithecine stage, it was still maintained to a greater extent than we currently see in modern human populations. The stress put on the male physique during hunting activities was such that muscularity, joint reinforcements and general skeletal robustness were all developed to a degree not now encountered. However much stealth and cunning were used in tracking and stalking, the moment inevitably came when the hand-held spear was thrust into the intended victim. Now the chances that a ton or so

Pithecanthropine sexual dimorphism shown between a female (OH 13) and a male (OH 9) from the middle of Bed II at Olduvai Gorge, Tanzania. The broad base of the male skull provides an attachment area for the muscles of a neck that was very much stouter than that of the female.

of Pleistocene buffalo or whatever will quietly and obligingly expire at the first jab of a hunter's spear are small indeed. In the twitching and thrashing of wounded prey, it is certain that, during the Early and Middle Pleistocene, the hunters regularly got banged around a bit. Torn knee ligaments, broken bones, dislocations or cracked skulls could easily have had fatal consequences. Not surprisingly, we see the development of bony and muscular reinforcement in the skeletons of the male hunting hominids. Skull walls and long bone shafts are thicker than before or since, joints are expanded and reinforced, and the muscle markings suggest great bodily strength.

The most complete picture of the Pithecanthropine stage is based upon the fragments excavated from Choukontein, just southwest of Peking (Peiping), China, between the late 1920's and the beginning of the Second World War in the Far East. In terms of the Pleistocene glacial sequence, these date from the late second glaciation or early second interglacial. They were roughly contemporary with the remains which Dubois, and later von Koenigswald, discovered in Java and which give their name to the phase. Actually, von Koenigswald's Modjokerto infant and his so-called Pithecanthropus IV come from the Djetis layer underlying the Pithecanthropus-containing Trinil series, and may be comparable in age to the early Pithecanthropines of Africa.

Aside from the expansion of the brain, the other major contrast between the Australopithecines and the Pithecanthropines can be seen in the dentition and its supporting facial skeleton. Pithecanthropine front teeth are slightly larger, but the molars had reduced to the point where they were within the upper limits of the modern range of variation. With a significant

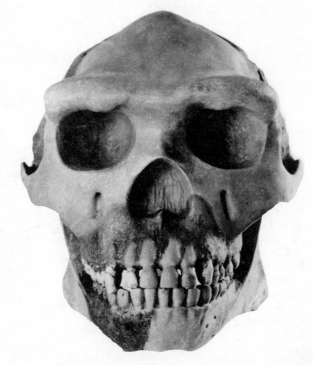

Pithecanthropus IV as reconstructed by Dr. Franz Weidenreich. The dark parts are original and the light, reconstruction. The whole back part (not visible) was preserved. Recent finds in Java and China have confirmed the accuracy of Weidenreich's reconstruction. (Courtesy of the American Museum of Natural History.) The individual was probably a male.

quantity of meat a regular part of the diet, the amount of chewing formerly necessary was considerably diminished. The amount of mastication necessary to reduce animal protein to digestible form is far less than is true for vegetable products. Ruminants are forced to chew, chew, and rechew their food so that a thorough mixture with salivary enzymes will assure its digestibility. A quick look at the molars of a cat, however, will demonstrate that shearing rather than crushing is their main function. For a carnivore, the main purpose of the molars is to reduce their food to swallowable size, since animal protein does not require extensive salivary enzyme action before it can start to be digested in the stomach. If our Pithecanthropines were eating significantly greater quantities of meat than their Australopithecine forebears, then they should have had less need for the greater crushing molars of the Villafranchian forms. With molar size free to vary, then the probable mutation effect could do its work, with the result that reduction took place. Critics may cry that this smacks of facile explanation, but, at the moment, no alternative suggests itself.

So far we have mentioned the use of cunning and stealth in hunting, but it seems likely that another basic approach was also used. The human adaptation to long-distance locomotion is actually fairly remarkable in its own right, although, considering the flabby physique of the average reader in his armchair, it is perhaps less easy to appreciate this than it should be. As an example of what a well-conditioned human being is capable of, one can cite the mode of hunting practiced even today by certain peoples. This involves literally walking one's quarry into the ground. South African Bushmen, American Indians, and Australian Aborigines are noted for this simple, if rather exhausting, technique. The hunter takes up the trail of a large herbivore and keeps it moving until out of sheer fatigue it can go no farther, at which

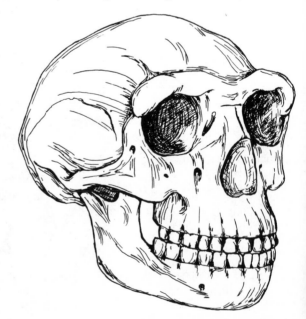

A composite reconstruction made under the direction of Franz Weidenreich and based upon the Pithecanthropine fragments found at Choukoutien, near Pekin. Originally called *Sinanthropus pekinensis.* The individual on which this was based was almost certainly female.

point the hunter moves in and dispatches it. The process may actually drag out over a number of days, involving a skill in tracking and a degree of patience and endurance difficult to conceive for the beneficiary of the technology of this mechanized age.

Two physiological facets aid the hunter in this form of activity. First, a large herbivore depends upon the ingestion of great quantities of food of relatively low nutritive value, which means that it has to spend a considerable portion of its lifetime eating. The hunter, on the other hand, fortified by occasional nibbles of concentrated nourishment in the form of dried meat products, nuts, and other high-quality edibles, can keep pushing on without stopping, prodding his quarry along just fast enough so that it does not have an adequate chance to replenish itself, and, in a couple of days, his patience will be rewarded. An interesting comment can also be made at this point. Human digestive physiology is quite different from that of the average nonhuman primate. The normal primate eating pattern is that of the nearly nonstop snack, which is paralleled by nearly nonstop elimination. Admittedly the fast food industry in the western world has shown how easy it is to reintroduce the old primate eating habits, but fortunately this has not been accompanied by a resumption of nonstop feces production. It would seem that the retooling job that made a primate into a hunter successfully accomplished a permanent change in its digestive physiology.

The second physiological fact involves the human ability to dissipate metabolically generated heat. Man, with his hairless skin richly endowed with sweat glands, can continue to function effectively throughout the heat of the day. The South African Bushmen capitalize on this fact by running down large quadrupeds in the middle of the day when the animals are prone to develop heat exhaustion if they attempt any continued rapid locomotion. In the tropics, mammalian life usually reposes in the shade during the hot part of the day. It is not without significance that all of the predatory carnivores which survive as a result of the active pursuit of prey engage in their maximum expenditure of energy in the relative coolness of the early morning or late afternoon and evening. Except for mad dogs, man alone goes out in the noonday sun—nor is this a peculiarity of the English, either. It would appear that the development of human predation long ago capitalized on the limitations which a coat of fur has placed upon mammalian activity during the heat of the tropical day, and one can suspect that the perfection of the hominid pelvis for long-distance walking was accompanied by the effective loss of human body hair. At the same time, the intensity of ultraviolet radiation poses something of a problem to the hairless tropic-dweller, since it greatly increases the chances of developing skin cancer. The solution is the development of a concentration of the protective pigment melanin. To follow up the train of these observations with a further speculation, it is possible to postulate that with the development of effective hunting techniques, somewhere in between the Australopithecine and the Pithecanthropine stages, people became hairless and black. Later we will account for the depigmentation which occurred in the background of some of the world's peoples, but at present it is sufficient to suggest that all of mankind passed through a heavily pigmented stage.

The deposits at Choukoutien reveal something else in the human behavioral repertoire which may be of great significance: fire. The charcoal accumulations which must have been built up over considerable periods of time suggest that the inhabitants of the local caves must have been able to control fire. The Choukoutien site is Middle Pleistocene in age, and recent excavations have shown that the use of fire had a comparable antiquity in other places—Israel, Hungary, southern France, and Spain. Doubtless when work is done on Middle Pleistocene sites elsewhere there will be further evidence for the use of fire. We still have no good idea how far back it goes and just when the control of fire became a part of the human cultural repertoire.

Since the subject of evidence for the human use of fire in prehistoric times is of some importance, it is worth exploring its implications. For one thing, such evidence is a boon to the prehistorian, since it means that the difficulties involved in discovering the remains of ancient habitations are greatly reduced. With the advent of fire, caves were inhabited by humans for the first time—a fact which greatly reduces the number of places the archaeologist has to investigate before getting results. Prior to the advent of fire, caves were studiously avoided at night by prehistoric hominids since they were more in the nature of traps than shelters. The keen visual sense which people inherited from their arboreal precursors, although remarkable in its acuity of color discernment and depth perception when light is provided, left (and still leaves) them relatively helpless in dim light, and practically disoriented in total darkness.

Fire is useful in three ways, and symbolic of a fourth phenomenon of considerable importance. It provides light, which extends the length of time during which a hominid can effectively operate. It provides nocturnal protection, which can convert the limiting confines of a cave into a safe area of refuge. And it provides warmth, which can enable a fundamentally tropical mammal to extend its range into colder climates normally closed to it. The final thing, that which fire symbolizes, is related to the reuse of an agreed-upon campsite. If the deposits at Choukoutien indicate an area which was intermittently used again and again, or even for a succession of days, then it is more than just likely that the users were capable of communicating time and place between each other. With this as a possibility, the ability of the group to divide up, agreeing to meet later at the camp, is also a possibility, and we must recognize in this the origins of the division of labor. Because of the physiological differences between males and females—the latter being charged with the care of infants and young—the most basic form of the division of labor is inevitably by sex, with the men concerned more specifically with the chase and the women concentrating on vegetable products and slow game. Even such a rudimentary division of labor as this can greatly increase the subsistence base of a foraging group; its effectiveness is evident in the fact that it is still characteristic of the remaining hunting and gathering peoples. Granting that this is rather a jump from the simple recognition of campsites via reused hearths, it nevertheless seems a legitimate interpretation to offer for a creature for whom specialized hunting activities had begun to play an increasingly important role in group subsistence.

Yet to be considered is the formal taxonomic designation of the Pithecanthropines and their geographic distribution. The controversy which raged over the status of the original Pithecanthropus around the turn of the century now belongs to history, although one or two professional scholars still would like to see it recognized as representative of a sideline which became extinct without issue. Although a great many anthropologists balk at accepting the Australopithecines for one reason or another, most are willing to regard the Pithecanthropines as genuine human beings who were ancestral to all later forms of humanity. As a result, the validity of the term *Pithecanthropus* as a formal generic designation has been questioned, and most authorities now regard them as belonging within genus *Homo*. The original specific designation is still considered tentatively valid, and many workers are quite happy in referring to the Pithecanthropines as *Homo erectus*.

A generation ago, when they were unchallenged as the oldest hominids known, and when they were recognized only in Java and China, there was a general feeling that Asia had been the cradle of mankind. Now, however, with Africa possessing the strongest claims to be the initial human homeland, there is much more willingness to view the Pithecanthropines as having spread throughout the area which the archaeological remains indicate was inhabited, rather than to regard them as having been restricted to one small province. New finds, and the reappraisal of an old one, provide confirmation for this suspicion. Robinson now regards the Swartkrans finds, which he and Broom originally called *Telanthropus*, as being a proper Pithecanthropine, and, although the brain case is lacking, the jaws and teeth would appear to prove him right. This was the first evidence discovered that showed the contemporaneity of an Australopithecine with an early Pithecanthropine. Further such evidence, although tantalizingly skimpy, was found at Olduvai Gorge, and, finally, it has been clearly and dramatically confirmed by the spectacular East Turkana finds made during the last five years.

One problem with trying to identify possible Pithecanthropines on the basis of jaws and teeth and not much more is the fact that they are indistinguishable from Neanderthal jaws and teeth. With no more skeletal evidence available, the nod as to which stage gets assigned is determined by dating. If the form is second glacial or second interglacial, jaws and teeth of Pithecanthropine size can be comfortably referred to the Pithecanthropine stage. An example is the famous Heidelberg mandible of 1907. The teeth correspond quite nicely to those discovered at Choukoutien, and, since the dating can be fixed at an interstadial of the second glaciation, it is reasonable to infer that Heidelberg represents the northwesternmost extreme of the Pithecanthropine range, just as Telanthropus may represent the southwesternmost extreme.

The Pithecanthropines at Olduvai and in the East Turkana area not only can be associated with a tool-making tradition that had developed straight out of the earlier Oldowan, but they occur in deposits that can be dated by radiometric means. At about a million and a half years old, they are older than all but one of the other Pithecanthropine collections. Some, but not all, of the Javanese finds appear to have a comparable antiquity. All of the others,

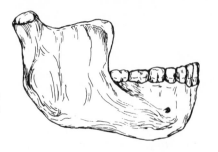

The Heidelberg jaw. Until the rash of discoveries of the last few years, this had been the only Pithecanthropine known in Europe.

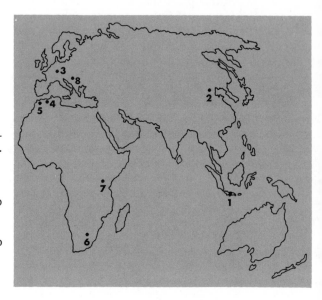

Sites of major Pithecanthropine discoveries. 1. Java. 2. Choukoutien. 3. Lantian. 4. Vertesszöllös (Hungary). 5. Heidelberg. 6. Arago (France). 7. Rabat (Morocco). 8. Ternifine (Algiers). 9. Bodo (Ethiopia). 10. East Turkana. 11. Olduvai Gorge. 12. Swartkrans.

Pithecanthropine skullcap from site LLK in Bed II of Olduvai Gorge, Tanzania. (Photo by Dr. L. S. B. Leakey, copyright National Geographic Society.)

however, including the Chinese and the increasing number of European discoveries, are no more than half that age, belonging in the Middle Pleistocene which only began 700,000 years ago.

As far as we have any reliable evidence, the Australopithecines were confined to the continent of Africa. Presumably the Pithecanthropines evolved

76

A biface from St.
Acheul in northwestern
France, the location
which gave its name to
a whole category of
middle Pleistocene
tools.

out of them there and only later spread out of their continent of origin. If the Javanese dates can be trusted, the spread to the east occurred quite rapidly, but the spread to the north, whether northwest (Europe) or northeast (China) took much longer to accomplish. Physiologically, people are still tropical mammals, and that must have been no less true for the early Pithecanthropines. Presumably after their subsistence pattern was developed in Africa, they were easily able to fill the diurnal hunting niche all the way across the tropics of the Old World. The spread north into what we curiously refer to as the "temperate" zone must have been possible only with the development of cultural adaptations that could compensate for the physiological limitations imposed by the tropical primate heritage. The development of clothing, of course, is one such compensation, and so is fire. It is interesting to note that both the Chinese and the European Pithecanthropines used fire, and it is tempting to suggest that this may have been the development that allowed the initial movement into those areas.

The initial occupation of previously uninhabited areas, whether the tropics of the Old World, or, later, the temperate zone, was obviously in the nature of an actual movement of people—even if this only involved the excess population of locally established groups budding off and inhabiting the next territory just a few miles away. However, once the habitable world was occupied, development from the Pithecanthropine stage to the succeeding ones was something that probably occurred gradually and simultaneously throughout the entire occupied world (rather than at one point, after which it would presumably spread by extinguishing the conservative local inhabitants, wherever they might be). After the initial Pithecanthropine spread, invasions of any note probably did not occur until the time of the great population imbalances and technological disparities that grew out of the food-producing revolution within the last 10,000 years.

The reason for this view can be seen in appraising the nature of the cultural adaptive mechanism. Cultural adaptations can and do diffuse with ease across the boundaries of specific cultures. The bow and arrow, for instance, diffused to most of the corners of the globe in a relatively short period of time, and the documented spread of the use of tobacco indicates a rate of diffusion and a disregard for cultural boundaries which is nothing less than

77

phenomenal. With the high degree of mobility and relative cultural uniformity functionally characteristic of the Lower Palaeolithic, any significant advance in hunting technique, food preservation process or the like must have diffused quite rapidly throughout the inhabited world—accompanied by the inevitable if not large leakage of genes across population boundaries as well. With the major forces shaping human evolution heavily influenced by major cultural adaptations, and with the latter effectively diffused, whatever their local origins, during the Lower Palaeolithic, then one can postulate relative similarity in the selective forces operating on human form. Similar forces would have produced similar evolutionary consequences in widely separate areas even without an accompanying slow genetic interchange, although this must have occurred as well. Starting with the Pithecanthropines, it is just possible that the diffusion of the cultural reasons for the specific physical changes which characterize the succeeding stages of human evolution were rapid enough so that the unity of the human species was maintained at any one time. Development from one stage to the next, then, would have proceeded at approximately the same time and the same rate throughout the inhabited world. The probability that a given population will be genetically more like its precursors in the same locality is of course greater than the probability that it will be genetically closer to groups in adjacent areas, and this allows for the development of regional peculiarities; however, at the same time, genetic material is continually being exchanged with adjacent areas. The result is that no human population has ever become different enough from the others to warrant taxonomic recognition.

Once again, observation of contemporary representatives of a hunting and gathering form of subsistence economy provide evidence which reinforces this suspicion. Among these people, exogamy—seeking mates from other unrelated groups—rather than endogamy or inbreeding is a virtually universal phenomenon. This greatly increases the possibilities not only for gene flow from group to group but also for information transfer as well. Not until local populations became sedentary, following the development of a food-producing subsistence economy, did group endogamy become a phenomenon to be reckoned with.

Eleven The
Neanderthal Stage

Of all the human fossils known, Neanderthals have generated the most public interest, serving as the prototype of the cartoon cave man. Somewhat ironically, now that the reading public has finally gotten to the point where it is willing to accept the hominid record as indicative of the course of human evolution, it is the professional anthropologists who have tended to become uneasy at the possibility of discovering a Neanderthal skeleton in the *sapiens* closet. However, if one accepts the Pithecanthropines as being a stage of human evolution, it is difficult to get from there to modern form without going by way of something which must be regarded as Neanderthal. Add to this the occurrence of Neanderthals in some quantities in the time immediately prior to the earliest reliably dated appearance of men of modern form, and the probability that the Neanderthals were the ancestors of ourselves is greatly increased.

Prehistoric research has been going on longer in western Europe than anywhere else, so it is no surprise to find that evidence for the evolutionary stage immediately prior to ourselves was first discovered and named in Europe and that more Neanderthal remains have been discovered there than anywhere

79

A Neanderthal. The classic "cave man," leopard skin, club, and all, dimly peering at a world which is largely beyond his comprehension. In fact, the Neanderthals probably had much more effective weapons and clothing, and there is reason to believe that they were at least as intelligent as modern men, if not more so.

else—starting with the first recognized specimen in 1856 which gave its name to the whole stage. In spite of this, it has taken the better part of a century for the various areas of interest which constitute the science of prehistory to mature. In the meantime, many discoveries have been made which could not be adequately treated because of the limitations of the times: stratigraphy was not controlled, faunal or cultural associations were not recorded, absolute dates could not be determined, and so on. Consequently, despite the quantity of Neanderthal material from Europe, virtually none of the major specimens can be precisely placed in time. The best we can do is associate them with the Mousterian tool-making tradition which, in turn, can be dated from approximately 35,000 years ago back to the beginning of the last glaciation or the late third interglacial some 100,000 years ago. However, direct dating of Neanderthal skeletal material has been made at two sites in the Middle East, one in Israel (Tabūn) and one in Iraq (Shanidar), and both agree, on the basis of C_{14} determinations, in assigning an age of 50,000 to 60,000 years ago. No fully developed Neanderthals are more recent than this, and the evidence suggests that many are much older, so it is fair to use this date as the tentative boundary for the most recent occurrence of the stage as a whole. For the beginning of the stage, specimens are few and fragmentary, and since they belong to a period too old to be dated by C_{14} and too young to be dated by K/A, there is more than a little uncertainty remaining.

To consider the form of the Neanderthals, one must start by dispensing with the hairy, slouching, bestial image, tramping through the Ice Age snow drifts clad only in a loincloth, and not quite able to stand erect. While there are minor differences in the pelvis of the known Neanderthals from those of modern man, there is no evidence to indicate that their posture was any less erect than that of ourselves. The human line has stood upright since the Australopithecine stage, and any attempt to inflict the Neanderthals with a "bent-knee" gait is simply a survival of the efforts on the part of early interpreters to view all aspects of Neanderthal anatomy as being "primitive" or ape-like. (This also involved the incorrect assumption that apes cannot straighten their legs at the knee.) From the neck on down, the only difference between Neanderthal and modern is the indications of generally greater ruggedness in Neanderthal joints and muscles. As with the Pithecanthropines,

80

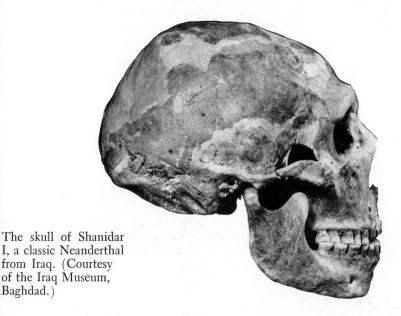

The skull of Shanidar I, a classic Neanderthal from Iraq. (Courtesy of the Iraq Museum, Baghdad.)

the demands imposed by a Middle Pleistocene hunting way of life continued into the early part of the Late Pleistocene. This is reflected in the continued existence of a powerfully developed skeleto-muscular system, particularly in the males. When one compares this to the modern situation, it is evident that this is more an average difference in degree rather than one in kind.

Above the neck, however, it is a different story. To be sure, the cranial measurements of some Neanderthals do not surpass those of some moderns, but there are other Neanderthals which present an array of dimensions which cannot be matched in recently living people. These revolve around the dentition and associated facial areas, where the Neanderthals do not differ functionally from the Pithecanthropines. All told, the Neanderthals are distinguished from the Pithecanthropines by the possession of brain cases of fully modern size, while they are distinct from moderns in the possession of Pithecanthropine dentitions and faces. In fact, the Neanderthal front teeth include the largest to be found in the whole picture of human evolution, although this may simply be due to the scarcity of specimens from the earlier stages.

Some people have regarded it as puzzling that the human brain should have attained full size 100,000 years ago or possibly more and remained the same ever since. The argument has been advanced that, if intelligence has survival value, more intelligence should have greater survival value. This, however, is failing to recognize that "survival of the fit" is a more appropriate expression than "survival of the fittest," and that the primary human adaptive mechanism is culture. When culture had developed to the point where the knowledge and traditions transmitted would confer an adequate chance of survival on any who could master it, the advantage of being yet more intelligent became relatively unimportant. Although one could argue that an innovator must have more intelligence than a person who is just able to master the culture in which he is brought up, it still remains true that the dullest member of a group benefits from the innovations of the brightest to an equal

81

extent, and that genetic endowments are passed on to the next generation with the proportions unchanged. In the face of such an explanation, it would be surprising to find an increase in cranial capacity during the last 100,000 years.

As a tentative definition of Neanderthal, this has been offered: "Neanderthal man is the man of the Mousterian culture prior to the reduction in form and dimension of the Middle Pleistocene face."

Actually, in any kind of strict sense, this is a somewhat tenuous generalization since, for all the impression of size and robustness that we get from perusing the faces and teeth of the "classic" Neanderthals of western Europe, it would appear that, even in them, the facial reduction that eventually produced what we recognize as modern form had already begun and proceeded to a considerable extent. This of course is just a reflection of what always happens when we try to cut up what is really a continuum into discrete categories. Even though facial reduction is already evident in the western European Neanderthals, we generally perceive their faces and teeth as being markedly larger than our own. It is this complex of premodern robustness that we can properly regard as Neanderthal form.

If the Neanderthals were characterized by the development of a modern-sized brain in a creature that still had a Middle Pleistocene body and face, then their predecessors late in the middle part of the Pleistocene ought to show signs that final expansion of the brain was taking place. This indeed is exactly what we find. The first of these late Middle Pleistocene finds to be recognized was the famous "Rhodesian" skull, discovered in 1921 deep in a mine shaft at Kabwe (then Broken Hill) in Zambia (then Northern Rhodesia). Brain size, at just over 1,250 cc., is well above the Pithecanthropine average of 1,000 cc. but below the modern male mean of 1,450 cc., although well within the normal modern range of variation. The face is a good, unreduced Middle Pleistocene representative, capped by a stupendous brow ridge. The neck muscle attachments likewise indicate that the head was set upon the body of a powerfully constructed Middle Pleistocene male. The date of the Rhodesian skull has been a matter for debate ever since it was found, but recently a new technique based upon the recemization of aspartic acid has been applied which places it at above 120,000 years ago, late in the Middle Pleistocene. All of this qualifies the Rhodesian find as an early representative of the Neanderthal stage in Africa.

In 1953, a similar skull vault, lacking the face, was found at Saldanha Bay near Hopefield, a scant hundred miles north of the Cape of Good Hope in South Africa. In the details of its form, it is strikingly similar to the Rhodesian skull. Furthermore, it was found associated with Mousterioid artifacts in an early Upper Pleistocene context. Even if all of this is not on a par with the abundant evidence from Europe, the dating, the artifacts, and the form provide strong support for the inferences concerning the existence of the Neanderthal stage in Africa.

A near duplicate of the Rhodesian skull was found by a group of cave explorers near the village of Petralona in northern Greece in 1959. The face and brow ridges suggest Pithecanthropine affinities. The cranial capacity, at

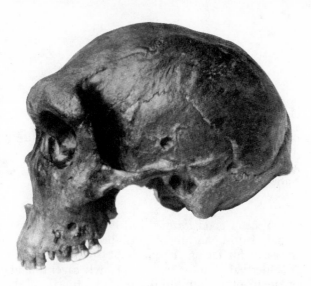

The Rhodesian skull, an African Neanderthal. (Courtesy of the American Museum of Natural History.)

1,220 cc., is halfway between the Pithecanthropine and Neanderthal, but lacking a date, it can be no more than suggestive.

The Far East has also obligingly yielded some crucial fossils. As with the initial discovery and the confirmation of the Pithecanthropine stage, Java has played the central role. Starting in 1931, 11 broken and faceless skulls were unearthed on the banks of the Solo River which recall the Pithecanthropines on the one hand and the Neanderthals on the other. The bones of the cranial vault are thick, the brow ridges and muscle markings are heavy, and the keeling along the mid-line, together with other details, looks more than faintly Pithecanthropine; however, the cranial capacity is halfway between Pithecanthropine and Neanderthal/modern and the date is considered to be just before the beginning of the Upper Pleistocene. All told, the Solo skulls appear to represent an evolutionary transition from the Pithecanthropine to the Neanderthal stage in the Far East. Together with other more recent skeletal remains, the evidence is most suggestive that the stage-to-stage evolution occurred simultaneously in all parts of the inhabited world —Europe, Africa, Asia, and by inference the areas between. Further confirmation of a full Neanderthal in Asia is offered by the discovery in 1958 of the upper parts of the face and the forward part of a skull of good Neanderthal form at Mapa, some 300 miles north of Canton in China.

If what has been presented so far would seem to be an uncomplicated demonstration of the genesis of Neanderthal form from the preceding Pithecanthropines, we should consider why it is that so many have refused to accept it. Three European finds are frequently cited as contradicting this apparently straightforward scheme. These are the specimens from Steinheim, Swanscombe, and Fontéchevade, to name them in order of their discovery. The oldest of these "skulls" is the Swanscombe skull, which is considered reliably dated to the latter part of the second interglacial. The pieces of this skull were discovered in a gravel pit of the lower Thames River in southeastern England, with the three major fragments constituting the rear of the cranial vault being unearthed in 1935, 1936, and, by an almost impossibly

83

One of the Solo skulls, a Javanese candidate for the Neanderthal stage. (Courtesy of the American Museum of Natural History, New York.)

rare piece of good fortune, in 1955. At the time when the initial pieces were found, British anthropologists, because of their long-standing lack of enthusiasm for facing the possibility that modern humanity may have had a Neanderthal ancestor, were desperately eager to find evidence for the existence of "men" of modern form at an earlier time level than that attributable to the Neanderthals. As a result, modern features were stressed whenever possible, and, in the case of Swanscombe, with the all-important facial parts missing, opinions concerning its status could be promoted without much risk of encountering solid objections from any quarter whatsoever. By default, then, Swanscombe has been regarded as modern ever since.

Despite the fact that the back end of the skull is relatively nondiagnostic in the assessment of the major distinguishing characteristics of evolutionary stage, there are some features which generally accompany those of diagnostic significance, and it is not without interest to discover some of these on the Swanscombe skull. For instance, the greatest width is far back and low down on the skull, and the skull height is remarkably low in proportion to it. The width across the occipital bone alone is greater than 99.9 percent of comparable modern skulls, and the bones are remarkably thick. There are other indications as well which locate the Swanscombe skull right in the middle of the characteristic Middle Pleistocene range of variation, but, lacking the crucial frontal bone and attached facial parts, we are not at liberty to do more than suspect that these parts may well have agreed with the indications of the vault. Unequivocal interpretation of Swanscombe is not possible, but, in marked contrast to the majority of the claims put forward on its behalf, it most certainly provides no evidence whatsoever for the existence of men of modern form in the Middle Pleistocene.

The Steinheim skull, found two years earlier in a gravel pit near Schiller's birthplace, not far from Stuttgart in west Germany, would at first consideration seem to be a more promising subject for interpretation than the Swanscombe skull. The date is roughly the same, being late second interglacial or early third glacial, and the skull is relatively complete, with much of the face preserved. Yet the arguments surrounding the attempt to establish its significance show no sign of diminishing. The skull is small and low, with a cranial capacity of approximately the Pithecanthropine average; the brow ridge is a formidable bony bar, but the back is rounded and smooth, suggesting modern form; the third molar is markedly reduced. Although the modern form of some of the other parts of the face has also been stressed, there are

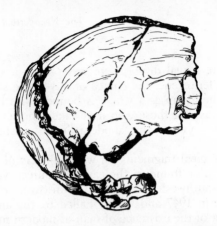

The Swanscombe skull viewed from the right side.

two principal difficulties in the way of definitive interpretations. First, the whole lower front part of the face is missing, leaving only the molars and one premolar at the rear of the dental arch. This is particularly regrettable since the most crucial features distinguishing modern from Middle Pleistocene morphology are those centered upon the forward end of the dental arch. The second difficulty lies in the distortion which the skull has undergone. The whole left side of the skull is crushed towards the mid-line, reducing the width of the base to less than that ever.recorded for a normal modern individual (where the width of the base tends to be less than for Middle Pleistocene individuals in the first place). The palate has been reduced in width, and the whole of the facial skeleton has been pushed slightly back underneath the skull. As a result of the missing and distorted aspects, it is evident that no unequivocal judgment can be made. Yet, with its small cranial capacity and heavy brow ridge, it can tentatively be regarded as belonging somewhere between the Pithecanthropines and the Neanderthals.

In the case of both Swanscombe and Steinheim, there is another aspect that has rarely been given due consideration. Both of these were female and therefore lacked the bony reinforcements and evidences for heavy muscle attachments that are so prominent on Middle Pleistocene male skulls. In a

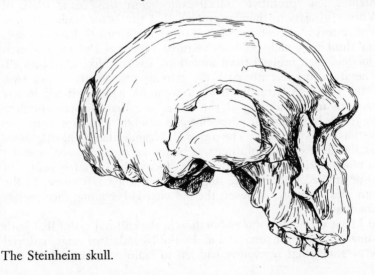

The Steinheim skull.

population where sexual dimorphism was pronounced, as it was during the middle of the Pleistocene, the choice of any single skull to characterize the appearance of the group as a whole is bound to be misleading. Such would seem to be the case for those who have taken the female form of Steinheim and Swanscombe to show that modern "man" existed before the Neanderthals.

The other principal fragments for which the cry of "ancient moderns" has been raised are those found in the cave at Fontéchevade in the Department of Charente in southwestern France. The discovery of pieces of two human skulls was made in 1947 and widely hailed by the anthropological world as proof at long last of the existence of man of modern form back in the Middle Pleistocene. Closer examination of the circumstances of the discovery and their nature, however, reveals a monumental amount of confusion. As it turns out, one of the skull fragments was not found *in situ* but in the laboratory where the block of material containing it had been brought for dissection at greater leisure. This fragment includes the section of a skull towards the medial part of the left eye-socket, between the eyes, and rising a short distance up the forehead. From what one can see, it is apparent that no heavy brow ridge was present, but, also from what one can see, there is no assurance that the fragment came from an adult. It is just as consistent to regard it as a juvenile from a population among which heavy brow ridges developed during adolescence.

The second Fontéchevade fragment includes the better part of the top of the cranial vault of what was apparently an adult; however, the diagnostic frontal and basal parts are missing, the piece is crumbly, and so much doubt clings to the attempts to project a reconstruction from the available parts that it would be far better to put the finds aside until more complete evidence is discovered. Certainly, at the moment, the only reason for stressing the dubiously "modern" features of Fontéchevade (or Swanscombe or Steinheim for that matter) is the desire which so many authors apparently have to find something less "primitive" which came before the Neanderthals of the last (Würm) glaciation, thereby proving that the latter could not possibly be the ancestors of recent mankind. This desire seems to have its roots in a trend of thinking which becomes alarmed whenever the suggestion is raised that modern man evolved from something less man-like than himself.

In the generation just recently past, the extreme proponents of this view denied ancestral status to virtually all fossil hominids which differed in any way from modern man, claiming at the same time that the true modern ancestor had yet to be found, or advancing the candidacy of now one, now another questionable specimen. The original Neanderthaler, having been found just at the time when evolution was becoming a major issue, was the subject of so much critical suspicion that, even today, the lingering vestige of this tends to be applied to the whole stage to which it gave its name. In the absence of any clear support, however, the old view is becoming increasingly difficult to maintain.

Now if, as I have claimed, it was elaboration in the cultural realm that both improved human chances for survival and, by the Neanderthal stage, reduced the selective pressures that previously had led to brain size increase, then it is worth paying some attention to the cultural remains themselves, and the implications which they contain.

The term Mousterian comes from the village of Le Moustier in south-western France where the type site is located. Tools of Mousterian form are distributed throughout western and southern Europe, south through the Balkans, east into the Middle East, and northeast through the Crimea, the Caucasus, and Uzbekistan. Throughout this whole area, which one could call a Mousterian culture area, there was a series of bands possessing related cultures between which similar culture elements maintained circulation. Local differences in details of typology and technique of manufacture persisted, but all these subcultures possessed the same functional tool categories: scrapers, points, and knives.

Scrapers indicate a concern for the preparation of animal hides, which is reasonable for people living in a subarctic climate. It used to be thought that effective clothing was not developed until the ensuing Upper Palaeolithic, with the invention and manufacture of bone needles, but there is no reason to deny the Neanderthals the use of skin clothing just because they had no needles: wrapped clothing bound on by thongs was utilized by the poorer peoples of Europe right up to recent historical times. Certainly the Neanderthals must have been doing something with the skins they prepared, and it is reasonable to suppose that the manufacture of clothing was one such thing.

The Mousterian points, made on flakes of a variety of sorts, evidently were frequently hafted, and the inference can be made that spears were being so tipped. Whether these were thrusting spears or throwing spears we have no way of knowing, but they obviously played an important role in the Neanderthal way of life. One might make the comment that the complex and precisely coordinated activities associated with throwing is a uniquely human phenomenon, no other animal having attained any degree of effectiveness in this practice at all. Possibly this is symbolized by the Mousterian point, but there is no way of proving it, however tempting it may be to add this to the evidence for increased hunting efficiency by the Neanderthals.

The onset of the last glaciation must have increased the problem of simple survival for the inhabitants of the northern portions of the Old World. Survival chances obviously would be improved as people increasingly attempted to manipulate and shape the natural world confronting them. There are two things that indicate an increasing concern for manipulative behavior among the Neanderthals. One is the heavy rounded wear that appears on their front teeth. Not only that, the front teeth reach the maximum size that they achieve during the course of human evolution, evidently in response to the selective pressures that favored the development and maintenance of that anatomical manipulative device, the original built-in. This stress on the survival value of manipulative behavior can also be seen in the proliferation of special categories of stone tools, a development that was stressed still further in the ensuing Upper Palaeolithic.

Before the onset of the last (Würm) glaciation, the representatives of genus *Homo* were unable to cope with a subarctic environment. Consistent with their African area of origin, humans have remained physiologically tropical animals to this day. The ability to invade and exploit other environ-

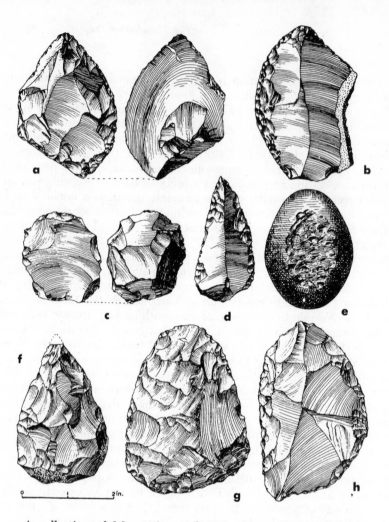

A collection of Mousterian tools. *a,b*, side-scrapers (racloirs), *c*, disc-core, and *d*, point, from rock-shelter at Le Moustier near Peyzac (Dordogne); *e*, small anvil or hammerstone (pebble of ferruginous grit), Gibraltar caves; *f*, hand-axe from Le Moustier; *g*, hand-axe (chert), and *h*, oval flake-tool (flint), from Kent's Cavern, Torquay. *a–d*. Typical Mousterian; *f*, Mousterian of Acheulian tradition; *g, h*, of Acheulo-Levalloisian tradition. (By permission of the Trustees of the British Museum of Natural History.)

ments is a product of specializations in the cultural adaptive mechanism. Until the late third interglacial, however, this cultural adaptive mechanism was not well enough developed to compensate for human physical inadequacies to the extent of allowing people to survive in a really chilly area. The onset of the preceding glaciations then forced people out of the increasingly inhospitable parts of what had formerly been the temperate zone. Climatic changes produced by the onset of glacial conditions were most extreme at the western end of the Old World temperate zone, where the Alps acted like

88

an enormous refrigerator and cooled off the whole of Europe. Scandinavia added to this general chilling and contributed to the continental ice sheet, which moved south across the Baltic, blanketing the northern edge of continental Europe and much of the British Isles. Since the most extreme climatic changes in the Old World focussed at the European end of the range, it is reasonable to expect that the greatest population dislocations occurred there as well.

By the time of the onset of the Würm, however, the pre-Neanderthal level of cultural attainment was just high enough so that, with some modifications, it allowed people to remain in the more northern unglaciated parts of Europe, southern Russia, and the Middle East, and to take advantage of the abundant food supply represented by the great numbers of large Pleistocene mammals which thrived there. Culturally, this represents a kind of forced adaptation which took place in the western reaches of the north temperate zone, with the consequence that, for the first time since the Australopithecine stage, there was a marked difference in the cultural adaptations of otherwise similar peoples in different parts of the world.

Archaeological evidence from Africa suggests that some of the technological inventions of the Mousterian culture area diffused to the south, where such things as spear points were made according to local techniques of manufacture, but the whole complex which bears the label Mousterian remained in the north. There are some suggestive tool fragments in China and Mongolia, but by-and-large it would appear that no such development occurred there or in India. Accident of circumstances, then, gave the inhabitants of the area from Europe through the Middle East a technological head start over the other peoples of the world, and, with many modifications, the effect of this fortuitous set of events continues to the present day.

There was another cultural development at this time that was eventually to change the face of humanity in a literal sense. This was the beginning of culinary elaboration. We are not really attuned to thinking of gastronomy as a Neanderthal invention, and perhaps it would be stretching things a bit to make such a claim, but there is reason to believe that they were the ones who pioneered the use of cooking as a regular means of preparing food.

The "hearths" that appear in Mousterian sites were obviously different affairs from those used for open camp fires. Even after 50,000 years, the swirl of ashes and fire-blackened cobbles of a Mousterian hearth preserves a depth that indicates that in original form it had been more than just a surface phenomenon. In fact, the remains look remarkably like those of recently used earth ovens (roasting pits) of the kind still relied on in modern Polynesia and elsewhere. Their construction and use go like this: a pit is scooped out in the ground, a collection of fist-sized rocks is placed in the bottom, and a fire is built over the rocks; when the fire has consumed the fuel, the rocks are raked aside and the object to be cooked is placed in the bottom of the pit; the rocks are then pushed up against and over the food item, the whole is covered with a skin, or leaves or grass (or burlap, today) and dirt shoveled over everything. The overlying dirt provides an insulating blanket that keeps the heat within, and, with the heat provided by the rocks, the food steams in its own juices. Aficionados of the New England clambake or the Polynesian luau claim that there is no tastier way of preparing food. The results are not only delicious, but they are also remarkably tender.

While we tend to stress the relationship between cooking and the taste of our food, the basic reason why cooking is practiced has very little to do with taste. The reason that things are cooked is to render them edible and digestible. Many vegetable foods cannot be handled by the digestive system until they are chemically altered by the application of heat. Meat, on the other hand, does not have to be cooked initially to make it digestible, but after it has been sitting around for a while, particularly if it is not refrigerated, then it has to be cooked quite thoroughly or else it can cause considerable gastric distress to say the very least. Spoiled meat was probably not much of a problem for the Palaeolithic hunters during their glacial winters, but frozen meat almost certainly was. Even the hungriest of Neanderthal bands could hardly have consumed more than a fraction of a woolly rhinoceros before the rest of it froze. Without some way of thawing it, then, the bulk of its meat would have been unusable. In order to make use of the majority of the meat acquired by their hunting efforts, the Neanderthals of the last glaciation must have used some sort of regular cooking techniques. The earth oven method is not only a logical candidate, but it is the one that makes the most efficient use of fuel. And then there are those Mousterian "hearths" that look so remarkably like the remains of earth ovens. Surely this is more than meaningless coincidence.

Now the regular use of such a form of cookery would substantially reduce the amount of chewing necessary. With this being the case, we could predict that the probable mutation effect would then be allowed to operate without detriment and that dental reduction would shortly ensue. Again, this appears to have been the case. The largest collection of Neanderthal teeth is from the site of Krapina in Jugoslavija, which comes from the time just before the onset of the last glaciation. The molars are fully as large as those of the Pithecanthropines a million years earlier and the front teeth, reflecting the importance of their manipulative function, are even larger. But by the time of the Würm Neanderthals of Belgium and France, maybe forty-thousand years more recently, tooth reduction had proceeded to such an extent that, in gross size, they were closer to the average for Upper Palaeolithic populations. It would appear that the reductions that served to produce modern face form had already begun in the Neanderthal groups in the northern parts of their area of occupation and it may very well have been the result of their innovative culinary practices.

As with the advance from the Australopithecine to the Pithecanthropine stages, the development from the Pithecanthropine to the Neanderthal stage took place throughout the inhabited parts of the Old World at the same time. This presents something of a contradiction if we use a strict interpretation of Mousterian in our definition of the Neanderthal stage, because of the limited geographical distribution of what is technically included within the term Mousterian. Some better cultural term should be used for the purpose of defining Neanderthal as a world-wide stage. Some archaeologists have used the term Middle Palaeolithic to differentiate it from the Upper and Lower Palaeolithic, and this term might be preferable were there not so much

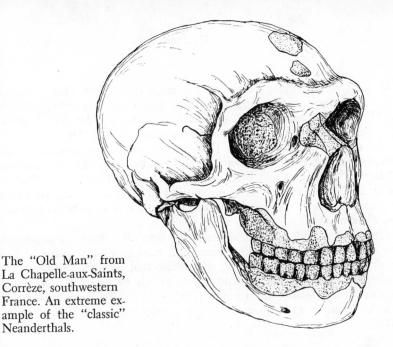

The "Old Man" from La Chapelle-aux-Saints, Corrèze, southwestern France. An extreme example of the "classic" Neanderthals.

archaeological opposition. Perhaps the term "Mousterioid" might be used provisionally to include the Mousterian proper and all the similar cultures based on flake technology.

As an indicator of the geographical distribution of the Neanderthal stage, human skeletal material is almost better than the archaeological record—far less complete of course, but more clearly indicative. The European skeletal material is represented by the original Neanderthaler, the Spy remains, the "Old Man" of La Chapelle-aux-Saints, skeletal remains from La Ferrassie,

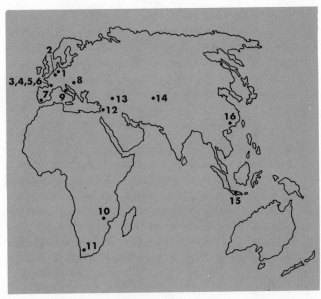

Neanderthal distribution as represented by the locations of some of the more important discoveries. 1. Neanderthal. 2. Spy. 3. La Chapelle-aux-Saints. 4. Le Moustier. 5. La Ferrassie. 6. La Quina. 7. Gibraltar. 8. Krapina. 9. Saccopastore. 10. Broken Hill (Rhodesian Man). 11. Saldanha. 12. Mount Carmel. 13. Shanidar. 14. Teshik Tash. 15. Solo. 16. Ma-Pa.

91

Gibraltar, La Quina, Monte Circeo, and a great many more less complete finds. Relatively abundant remains have been discovered in southern Russia and the Middle East, with perhaps the most exciting (and datable) remains coming within the last decade from Shanidar cave in Iraq. The most complete skeleton is the female from the Tabūn cave on Mount Carmel in Israel, which shows that sexual dimorphism was still pronounced, although perhaps just a little less so than it had been during the Middle Pleistocene. Skeletal remains of the Neanderthal stage from the rest of the Old World are much less abundant, although the available fragments allow the inferences of distribution to be made.

The foregoing should suffice to indicate the form, the dating, and the distribution of the Neanderthal stage. Since full modern cranial capacity had been attained, presumably indicating the intellectual capabilities equivalent to those of modern man, it would not be justifiable to regard the Neanderthals as specifically distinct from men of today. Formally, then, this makes them *Homo sapiens* with at most a subspecific appendage of *Neanderthalensis*.

Twelve The
Modern Stage

Forty years ago, the appearance of modern humanity would have been announced in phrases such as these: "Sweeping into Europe from out of the East came a new type of man, tall and straight, with strong but finely formed limbs, whose superiority is proclaimed in the smooth brow and lofty forehead, and whose firm and prominent chin bespeaks a mentality in no way inferior to that of ourselves. In this fine and virile race we can recognize our own ancestors who suddenly appear upon the scene and replace the degenerate and inferior Neanderthals, perhaps as a result of bloody conflict in which the superior mentality and physique of the newcomers tipped the balance. Whatever the cause, the lowly Neanderthals disappear forever and the land henceforth becomes the never-to-be-relinquished home of our own lineage, the creator of the culture which is our own patrimony, and the originator of what has been built to the heights of Western civilization."

While this paragraph is pure invention, it nevertheless captures some of the flavor of the interpretive accounts of human evolution written a half century ago. Their appeal to the imagination of the literate world was immense. In the first place, the reference to an Eastern origin strikes a powerful chord

93

in the mind of the Western reader who is conditioned from infancy to regard all that is civilized and sanctified in antiquity to have had its origins "in the East." To these holy overtones are added the implications of the mysterious Orient. But this is just the beginning. The appeal to the lofty brow, often accompanied by explicit statements concerning the degree of development of the frontal lobes of the brain, caters to a folk belief, dating from the phrenology of the early nineteenth century and still current, that this is somehow indicative of superior mental ability. The portrayal of our own ancestors in terms which correspond to the stereotyped picture of European masculinity—prominent chin, straight-limbed, tall, to which hints of blue eyes and fair hair are often added—stimulates a conscious pride in belonging to such a line. To complete the scene with all the components of a good old-fashioned melodrama, the Neanderthals are brought in as the embodiment of the villain. They are depicted as strong and dangerous, although dwarfed and physically inferior, crafty but not really intelligent, hairy and doubtless violent and bestial. In spite of adversities, good prevails and evil is vanquished, with the Neanderthals disappearing forever.

As an added attraction to our already potent little drama, all direct relationship between the Neanderthals and the invading moderns is either flatly denied, or pushed so far back in time that it is lost in the mists of remote antiquity—which of course means that even people who are uneasy about accepting an evolutionary account of modern human origins can accept this story without any qualms. Dazzled by such dramatics, few people were disturbed by the total lack of any reason for such an invasion, of any source for the invaders, or of any perspectives on what they evolved out of and why. Analogous to the legend in which Athena sprang fully armed from the brow of Zeus, so it would seem that early twentieth-century prehistorians solved their headache concerning human origins by projecting a modern human

An Upper Palaeolithic hunter, the first of the modern stage. Neatly dressed and clean shaven, he strides forth confidently to fulfill the destiny which his clear vision tells him is to be his future. Actually, the archaeological evidence does provide support for the existence if not the invention of tailored clothing and compound weapons in the Upper Palaeolithic, but the lofty brow and "noble" expression are quite unwarranted idealizations.

stereotype, fully formed, from their own inner consciousness smack into the early Pleistocene and thereby created their own anthropological mythology.

It scarcely needs to be said that this book does not subscribe to such a myth-like view. Recognizing that it is essentially an expression of faith—faith in a process—the attitude behind this presentation is based on the assumption that the hominid fossil record can be comfortably accommodated within the framework of standard evolutionary theory as it is applied to the human world. Noting that the Neanderthals have an antiquity demonstrably greater than that of moderns and that nothing but modern skeletal material is evident since about 35,000 years ago, it is important to place both stages within the same evolutionary framework. If, as is claimed, the Neanderthals simply evolved into modern form, then structurally and temporally intermediate forms should be apparent, and some rationale should be available to account for the change. Fortunately (for the present scheme), both can be produced.

In the early 1930's, excavations in the rock shelter of Skhūl on the slopes of Mount Carmel in Israel (near the cave of Tabūn which yielded a full-scale Neanderthal) produced a population of what can be called Neanderthaloids. That is, they recall genuine Neanderthalers in many respects, but in other features deviate in the modern direction. The dentition and the entire surrounding face has been somewhat reduced, leaving the forehead and sides of the cranial vault more vertical and producing the first vestiges of a genuine chin—formerly regarded as the "hallmark" of modern form. Reductions in the robustness of ribs, long bones, and other aspects of the postcranial skeleton also show modification in the modern direction. For many years the suggestion was made that the Mount Carmel material was third interglacial, which would have made it older than the full Neanderthals dated to the fourth glaciation in Europe and recently confirmed at Shanidar in Iraq. To explain this mixture of traits, the interpretation was advanced that the people of Mount Carmel were hybrids between a fully Neanderthal group, represented by Tabūn and now Shanidar, and a fully modern group for which such vague fragments as Swanscombe or even the Piltdown fraud were advanced. Recently, however, the difficulties which such an approach encounters have been altered by the reappraisal of Mount Carmel dating. By C_{14} the Tabūn skeleton has been shown to be around 60,000 years old, and the Skhūl material has been placed at about 35,000 years ago. This makes the Skhūl population intermediate in time as well as in form between the Neanderthal and modern ends of the spectrum and eliminates all need for theories involving hybridization, with their attendant difficulties.

A few other isolated finds of intermediate character also exist, and the Neanderthal origin of modern man is further supported by the presence of a fair proportion of dissociated Neanderthaloid characteristics in the earliest clearly Upper Palaeolithic populations. The first such Upper Palaeolithic population to be discovered was the Cro-Magnon group, found less than a decade after Darwin's *Origin* appeared. Occasionally the term Cro-Magnon is applied to designate the early moderns as a stage, and occasionally it and other terms (Grimaldi, Combe Capelle, Chancelade, etc.) are used to designate separate supposed "races" of modern people in the Upper Palaeolithic. This

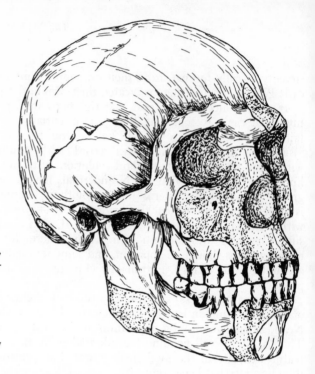

A Neanderthaloid skull, Skhūl V, the best preserved representative from a group of ten individuals found in a rock shelter on the slopes of Mount Carmel, Israel, in the early 1930's.

would seem premature, since it is most unlikely that four or more separate races existed in southern France (where these representatives were found) during the Upper Palaeolithic. For the present, these can all be referred to as the Upper Palaeolithic representatives of the Modern stage. As has already

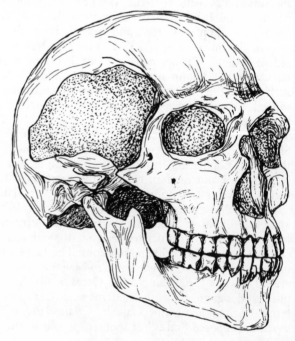

An Upper Palaeolithic skull, Předmost III, a male from a large collection excavated in western Czechoslovakia in the late nineteenth and early twentieth centuries. A lingering robustness of brow ridges, facial skeleton, and muscle markings recall earlier conditions in human evolution.

96

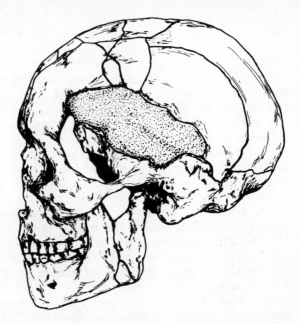

An early Upper Palaeolithic skull from Mladeč in Czechoslovakia showing more than traces of Neanderthal form in the area of neck muscle attachments and in the brow ridges. The original was destroyed by German soldiers in the Second World War. Pictured is Mladeč V, drawn from a cast.

been mentioned, the chief physical differences between the Neanderthals and the moderns is to be seen in the development of the dentition, its supporting facial architecture, and related parts of the skull, plus certain aspects of general skeletal development and musculature. In all these features, the moderns show a marked degree of reduction from the Neanderthal state, although the early Upper Palaeolithic representatives are markedly more robust in these features than is generally true for modern man today.

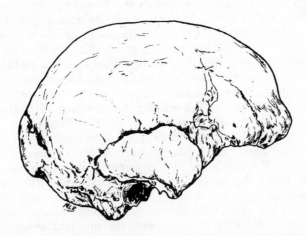

The Combe Capelle skull, an early Upper Palaeolithic find from southern France showing some Neanderthaloid traces in the brows and in the tooth-bearing part of the jaws. The original was destroyed when an American bomb landed on the museum where it was stored in Berlin during the Second World War. Drawn from a cast.

Several generations of scholars have noted that the appearance of modern form is correlated with the appearance of Upper Palaeolithic tool-making traditions which represent an advance in complexity over the Mousterian comparable to the advance which the Mousterian showed over the Lower Palaeolithic. Refinements in tool-making are signalled by the technique of preparing flint cores so that long narrow spalls, technically called *blades,* can be detached. This increases the number of tools which a given amount of raw material can yield, and, further, the tools thus produced are worked into a greater variety of functionally distinct forms than was previously the case. Points, knives, and scrapers are refined, and to these are added a variety of gouging tools called burins. Also notable is the appearance of an extensive bone industry—harpoon points, awls, and needles with eyes in them. With the small flint spear points and harpoon heads, it is apparent that hunting now definitely uses the technique of hurling projectiles at prey. This is further supported by the appearance of spear-throwers, *atlatls,* which, by acting as an extension of the arm, significantly increases the power of propulsion and adds to the effective range over which a spear can operate. Certainly the vast quantities of animal remains found in Upper Palaeolithic sites attest to the effectiveness of hunting techniques, and one can assume that a higher level of social cooperation in game drives and trapping procedures must have existed as well. Finally, from the needles it has been inferred that shaped and sewn—tailored—clothing was being made.

Initially, the Upper Palaeolithic appears in the same area where the Mousterian had flourished before it. The same caves are utilized as shelters and the same kinds of animals are being hunted. All told, it can be regarded as a refined outgrowth—a culminating perfection—of the cold-climate adaptation of which the Mousterian represents the beginning. New technological items have been added, although many are simply refinements of the cruder Mousterian counterparts, but the basic dimensions of life are not radically different. The difference is more one of relative efficiency than of kind.

Survival in the north temperate zone depended upon the cultural developments which started in the Mousterian and continued without break in the Upper Palaeolithic. Since cultural changes, even at the Australopithecine level, represent alterations in the selective forces which affect the hominids involved, one should expect to find some sort of reflected change to have occurred in the anatomy of the beneficiaries. One of the most obvious differences which set apart the Mousterian and the Upper Palaeolithic from the preceding Lower Palaeolithic is the appearance of a profusion of special cutting tools. From the bifaces (hand axes) and crude flakes of the pre-Würm cultures, one goes to the variety of points, scrapers, and knives of the Mousterian and the even more elaborate technology of the Upper Palaeolithic. Obviously the ability to manipulate the surrounding world has been one of the prime factors in the successful survival of the human line, but equally obvious is the fact that a technological basis for any extensive manipulating did not exist prior to the Mousterian.

From the extraordinary wear visible on the front teeth of the Neanderthals and their predecessors, one can suggest that it was the dentition which bore the brunt of the finer manipulations and itself served as a sort of general

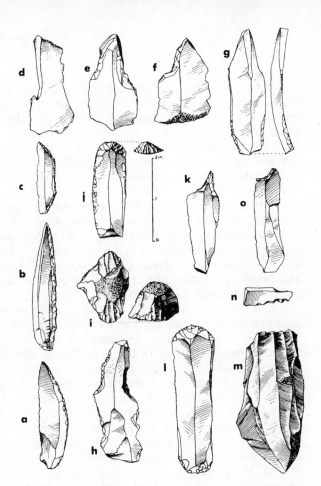

Upper Palaeolithic flint tools. a and b, "knife points"; d, e, f, and g, gravers or burins; i, j, l, and o, scrapers; k, a piercer; c, h, and n, miscellaneous tools; m, a core from which blades have been struck. (By permission of the Trustees of the British Museum [Natural History].)

all-purpose tool—the original built-in. With the appearance of an adequate cutlery at the beginning of the Mousterian, the significance of possessing large and powerful front teeth was substantially decreased. This would have allowed the probable mutation effect to operate throughout the early Würm, resulting in the reduction of the forward part of the dental arch and the supporting parts of the face. Furthermore, the process must have been speeded up as technological refinement advanced toward the Upper Palaeolithic level. In similar fashion, the continuation of the cookery traditions that began in the Mousterian relaxed the selective pressures that had formerly maintained a Middle-Pleistocene sized set of molars. The modern face, then took shape as a result of reductions at both the front and the back of the dental arch.

The significance of this change in tooth use can be appreciated if one considers for a moment the characteristic mode of eating of modern hunting and gathering peoples. Meat is not daintily manicured into bite-sized portions with knife and fork before ingesting; rather, a chunk is taken in the hand and thrust part way into the mouth, where it is held with the front teeth while being sawed off at lip level by means of a cutting implement. As practiced by modern hunters and a variety of peasants throughout the world, it is aided by the efficiency represented by metal knives, but even so the effect is sufficient to produce a substantial amount of flat wear on the incisors

99

and canines, resulting in the "edge-to-edge" bite characteristic of so many backward peoples. Before metallurgy, this form of tooth wear was more extensive, and one can just imagine the burden placed on the front teeth *before* the development of even an adequate *stone* cutlery.

The heavy wear apparent on the front teeth of many of the Neanderthals indicates that the burden was only gradually shifted from the dentition. This is reasonable, since the reduction of the full Neanderthal face is only halfway accomplished in the Skhūl population of Mount Carmel and is still incomplete in the early Upper Palaeolithic, and it suggests that the teeth were important for more than simply processing food. The curious rounding wear of Neanderthal incisors indicates that they were using their teeth to tan leather in a fashion similar to that of the modern Eskimo, which is consistent with the view presented above that they were utilizing skins for clothing. This brings up another area of cultural adaptation and leads to another suggestive if unproven speculation.

Recall that the development of a hairless and heavily pigmented skin was suggested for the hunters early in the Pithecanthropine stage. From this, one must assume that the early Neanderthals who first successfully adapted to the north temperate zone in the early Würm were dark brown or "black," as a correlate to man's generally tropical physiology. The use of clothing, among other things, was of great importance in the success of their adaptation, but one can suggest that it had an interesting if somewhat unexpected by-product. By covering the skin with clothes, the importance of the epidermal pigment melanin as an ultraviolet filter is drastically reduced, and, once again, the probable mutation effect operating over a substantial period of time would serve to reduce the structure whose importance had been decreased. The result is depigmentation, and it is of more than passing interest to note that, in general, those parts of the world where the amount of pigment in the human skin is at a minimum are also just those areas where Mousterian scrapers and Neanderthal teeth indicate that clothing has been utilized for the longest period of time. The picture evoked by a blond Neanderthaler is somewhat contrary to the usual stereotype, but it is quite possible that the invention of clothing by the northern Neanderthals of the early Würm was the source of the depigmentation phenomenon which allows some of the peoples of the world today to be described by the euphemism "white."

Many people have assumed that once modern form was achieved, evolution stopped and we shall live happily ever after, virtually unchanged. The truth, however, is quite otherwise. The changes that produced early modern out of Neanderthal form have continued in the same direction, and, if anything, have actually speeded up.

Late in the Pleistocene, the herds of large-sized game animals began to disappear. Some have suggested that the efficiency of the Upper Palaeolithic hunters had gotten so great that they were cropping the herds faster than they could reproduce. In any case, big game hunting became a less and less important aspect of human subsistence activities. Many an archaeologist, relishing the dramatic imagery conjured up by the Pleistocene mammoth hunters, has felt that the culture of the succeeding Mesolithic represented a "decline" from the heights of art and technology that had previously been achieved. Again, this simply is not the case. During the Mesolithic, netting and traps were developed which enabled people to exploit quantities of fish, small mammals and birds which had constituted only an insignificant resource when they could only be caught, if at all, one at a time. Furthermore, the development of mortars and pestles and other forms of grinding technology allowed the people of the Mesolithic to utilize an even more significant source of foods than had not been possible before, namely grain. With access to quantities of small game and the newly developed ability to use wheat, oats, millet, barley and other grains as staples, human population size underwent a sudden and dramatic increase. By the end of the Pleistocene 10,000 years ago, the use of grains as a subsistence base had advanced to the extent that they were being deliberately planted in the Middle East and probably in South China/Southeast Asia, and the gathering of the Mesolithic had been transformed to the full-fledged farming of the Neolithic. Shortly thereafter, the discovery and manufacture of pottery further reduced the already lessened survival value in the possession of a large and well-developed dentition. By using cooking pots, one can simmer one's food to drinkable consistency, at which point the edentulous can ingest their calories as easily as those who still possess a veritable Pithecanthropine dental arch. It is no accident that the populations with the smallest (and fewest) teeth in the world today are the ones associated with the areas where the Neolithic and preceding Mesolithic go back farthest in time.

With changes in the cultural adaptive mechanism suggested as being responsible for changes in face form and skin color, it should be possible to account for some of the major visible differences between the living peoples of the world in the same way,.and this is indeed the case, although to go into this in any detail is beyond the scope of this book. In the area where technological complexity has been having its impact for the greatest length of time, one would expect dental reduction to have proceeded to its greatest extent—and, as can be seen, these expectations are fulfilled. Using the same logic, one would expect the different degrees of dental development seen in India, Africa, Asia, the Americas, and Australia to be correlated with the length of time during which the relevant peoples have been enjoying the benefits of technological elaboration—and, again, expectations are fulfilled. The most striking example is that of Australia, where the facial form of the aborigines shows less reduction than any of the other modern human groups. Even within Australia, however, there is a remarkable north-south gradient. Mesolithic culture elements such as nets and seed grinders clearly came in from the north after the end of the Pleistocene. These altered conditions for the inhabitants, who had been living there for at least 40,000 years to such an extent that, at the time of contact with the incoming Europeans, tooth size of the northernmost aborigines had reduced to the level visible in the European Upper Palaeolithic. That reduction was less apparent towards the south where the incoming cultural elements presumably had an ever shallower time depth; therefore, by the time one gets down to the Murray River basin in southern Australia, tooth size had reduced only a little from the Middle Pleistocene level of the fossil Murray inhabitants, being, at least in the molar area, distinctly larger than for the "Classic" Neanderthals of western Europe.

Using the arguments developed above, one can suggest that the human diversity visible in the world today is largely a product of events which have occurred during the last 70,000 years or so. It is only during this time that the archaeological record yields clear signs of functional differentiation in the cultural adaptive mechanism. This, as has been suggested, was initiated by the survival problems posed by the periglacial areas. Solutions to these problems had a number of important consequences. One of these was the ability to thrive in the more northern areas which were opened up during retreats of the ice sheets. Following these north, people at the Upper Palaeolithic level spread across the whole vast plains area of the Old World and, at the eastern extremity, crossed the land bridge between Siberia and Alaska, producing the initial population of the New World—the only large-scale spread into previously unoccupied territory to have occurred since the expansion of the Pithecanthropine stage throughout the Old World tropics. It was people at a developed level of this same general stage of complexity who were able to domesticate plants and animals, thus assuring their food sources and creating the foundation for the still greater cultural disparities which followed. (This food-producing or Neolithic revolution occurred about 10,000 years ago in the Middle East and Southeast Asia and, independently, somewhat more recently in Middle America.) The effects of these various developments slowly diffused into other parts of the world, but a detailed discussion of the events involved and their impact is the subject of other books in this series.

One is tempted to speculate that the increasing technical and medical ingenuity of developing world culture will further reduce or suspend the adaptive significance of many other human features. Reduction of these features as a result of the probable mutation effect would then follow, and it is possible to suggest that people in the future will be somewhat puny and underendowed by today's standards. Each era creates its own values, however, and the Neanderthals might very well have had the same feelings about ourselves, could they have known that we, their remote descendants, should be so much

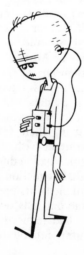

The man of the future (we are tempted to call him *Homo durabilis* or the man who endures). Although it is perhaps unwarranted to visualize our distant descendants as puny, balding, myopic, and toothless little men, there is reason to suspect that some such trends may occur. Note that in the previous stages of human evolution the cultural element symbolizing human adaptation was held in the hand of the man in question, whereas in this portrayal it is hung around his neck.

less robust than they. Perhaps our hypothetical man of 1,000,000 A.D.—should we call him *Homo durabilis,* "the man who endures"—will look back at the people of the twentieth century with feelings of repugnance and disgust. Tempting as such excursions may be, they do not properly belong in a book about the human past. In fact, they hardly belong to the realm of "science," and are included here only to lead the reader to realize that human evolution is not just something that occurred long ago—that it has been continual, that it is happening right now, and that it will go on in the future as long as people shall exist.

Epilogu

In summary, the figures on pages 105 and 106 present a supersimplified picture of the changes occurring in the entire span of human evolution, with their suggested causes. The second figure presents a record of hominid evolution seen only from the point of view of total tooth size. The vertical scale represents the average cross-sectional area in square millimeters of all of the teeth in the dental arch. The robust Australopithecines had obviously become very large of tooth prior to their extinction. The spread at the *sapiens* end of the graph reflects the fact that within the last 100,000 years, the teeth of some human populations have undergone a marked degree of reduction while those of others, the large-toothed southern Australian aborigines, had scarcely been altered at all.

It does not take an expert to recognize that more than the usual amount of speculation has been included in this book. The major pieces of evidence have been presented, and evolutionary theory has been considered. The speculation enters when theory rather than solid evidence has been used to support the interpretations offered, and it should be clearly recognized that this cannot constitute proof. As more fragments of human fossils are found in the years to come, the level of probability that one interpretation or another is correct will increase, but this is not proof either. Ultimately, it is impossible to "prove" the validity of any interpretation, but the theoretical consistency of the one presented here should be justification enough for its development. The future alone can decide the probability of its rectitude.

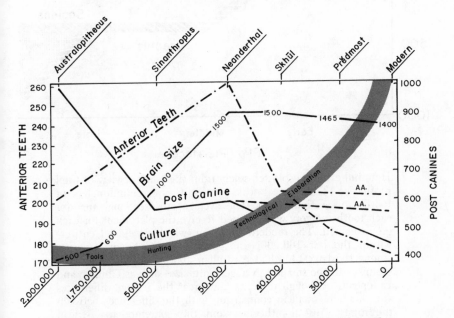

Graphic representation of the major changes which have taken place in human evolution and their association with changes in man's cultural adaptation. The figures for anterior teeth and post-canines represent the summed cross-section area of the teeth on one side of the upper dental arch. Brain size is in cubic centimeters. A. A. refers to modern Australian aborigines—note how close they are to the Neanderthaloids from Skhūl, Mount Carmel.

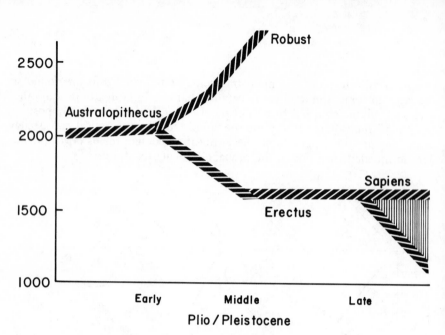

Hominid evolution plotted solely from the point of view of total tooth size. The vertical scale represents square millimeters of tooth cross-sectional area. The average cross-sectional area for each tooth category was summed to give the placement for each group named. The modern spectrum, which developed entirely within the last 100,000 years, shows the range of variation among the largest-toothed Australian aboriginal groups and the groups with the smallest average tooth size, such as Chinese and Europeans. Although it shows how great the average differences are, these are small in comparison with the differences between the robust Australopithecines and the contemporary· African Pithecanthropines. Each of the major changes on the graph correlates with major changes in adaptive strategy known for the groups indicated.

106

Selected References

Chapter One. There are a few books that will serve as background for interpretations of human evolution. The most complete and systematic of these is *Catalogue of Fossil Hominids, Part I: Africa,* K. P. Oakley and B. G. Campbell, eds. (London: The British Museum (Natural History), 1967), *Part II: Europe,* and *Part III: Americas, Asia, Australasia,* K. P. Oakley, B. G. Campbell, and T. I. Molleson, eds. (London: The British Musuem (Natural History), 1971 and 1975). An excellent discussion, although a very orthodox presentation, is available in W. E. Le Gros Clark's *The Fossil Evidence for Human Evolution: An Introduction to the Study of Paleoanthropology,* 2nd ed. (Chicago: University of Chicago Press, 1964). More recent but not fundamentally different treatment is presented in M. H. Day, ed. *Human Evolution* (New York: Barnes and Noble, 1973), and in Frank E. Poirier, *Fossil Evidence: The Human Evolutionary Journey,* 2nd ed. (St. Louis: Mosby, 1977). Dating of the evidence is treated in Kenneth P. Oakley's *Frameworks for Dating Fossil Man,* 2nd ed. (Chicago: Aldine Publishing Company, 1966).

Chapter Two. The background for the development of evolutionary thought is well portrayed by John C. Greene in *The Death of Adam: Evolution and Its Impact on Western Thought* (Ames: The Iowa State University Press, 1959). The triumph of the Darwinian point of view is well developed in Loren C. Eiseley's *Darwin's Century: Evolution and the Men Who Discovered It* (Garden City: Doubleday & Company, Inc., 1958). The different receptions to Darwin accorded by intellectuals in different countries is well presented in *The Comparative Reception of Darwinism*, Thomas F. Glick, ed. (Austin: University of Texas Press, 1974).

To gain some background in the attitudes of the French intellectual climate where Darwinian evolution has been resisted, see William Coleman, *Georges Cuvier, Zoologist* (Cambridge: Harvard University Press, 1964). This provides valuable perspective for understanding the interpretations offered in one of the widely used reference sources for human evolution, *Fossil Men*, by M. Boule and H. V. Vallois (New York: Dryden Press, 1957).

Chapter Three. The first and still one of the best attempts to interpret the skeletal remains of prehistoric human populations from a systematically evolutionary point of view is *Studien zur Vorgeschichte des Menschen* by Gustav Schwalbe (Stuttgart: E. Scheizerbart, 1906). Probably the best account of early discoveries and interpretations in English is Aleš Hrdlička's *The Skeletal Remains of Early Man*, Smithsonian Miscellaneous Collections No. 83 (Washington, D.C.: The Smithsonian Institution, 1930).

Chapter Four. The only explicit attempt to consider the impact of national intellectual traditions and the accidents of history on the interpretation of the evidence for human evolution is in "The fate of the 'classic' Neanderthals: A consideration of hominid catastrophism," by C. L. Brace in *Current Anthropology*, V, No. 1 (1964). Particularly interesting are the irate comments of the proponents of the traditional view which are printed following the main body of the article. This provides the basis for the view presented in Chapter 8 of C. L. Brace and Ashley Montagu's *Human Evolution: An Introduction to Biological Anthropology*, 2nd ed. (New York: Macmillan, 1977). The outrage of the orthodox to the view presented is well displayed by the review of the first edition (1965) by Robert W. Ehrich in *Human Biology*, XXXVIII, No. 3 (1966), and "More on the fate of the 'classic' Neanderthals," *Current Anthropology*, VII, No. 2 (1966).

Chapter Five. The accounts of those who contributed to the discoveries are particularly interesting. Franz Weidenreich reported some of his conclusions in *Apes, Giants and Man* (Chicago: The University of Chicago Press, 1946), but the most complete personal account is presented by G. H. R. von Koenigswald in *Meeting Prehistoric Man* (London: Thames & Hudson, 1956).

Chapter Six. Although some of the interpretations have been generally questioned, the most complete account to have been published of discoveries up to 1962 is Carleton S. Coon's *The Origin of Races* (New York: Alfred A. Knopf, 1962). For still more recent material see William Howells' *Evolution of the Genus Homo* (Reading: Addison-Wesley, 1973), and Russell H. Tuttle, ed. *Paleoanthropology: Morphology and Paleoecology* (The Hague: Mouton, 1975).

Chapter Seven. Standard evolutionary principles are well expressed in works such as Ernst Mayr's *Evolution and the Diversity of Life: Selected Essays* (Cambridge: Belknap Press of Harvard University Press, 1976), and the older but still excellent *The Major Features of Evolution* by George Gaylord Simpson (New York: Simon and Schuster, 1968, reprint of the 1953 edition).

The recent major advances in genetics are well presented in James D. Watson's *Molecular Biology of the Gene*, 3rd ed. (Menlo Park, California: Benjamin, 1976). Some unorthodox implications are suggested by Susumu Ohno in his *Evolution by Gene Duplication* (New York: Springer-Verlag, 1970). Capitalizing on these developments, and suggested as being of particular importance to human evolution, is the paper by C. L. Brace, "Structural Reduction in Evolution," *The American Naturalist*, XCVII, No. 1 (1963). The most recent attempt to resurrect the idea that neoteny somehow constitutes a key to our understanding of human form is that by Stephen Jay Gould in *Ontogeny and Phylogeny* (Cambridge: Harvard University Press, 1977).

Chapter Eight. One of the earliest explicit realizations of the behavioral significance of hominid body form was the unappreciated paper by Paul Alsberg, "The Taungs Puzzle: a Biological Essay," *Man*, XXXIV, No. 179 (1934).

For specific treatment of hominid ecology, tool use, behavior, and cultural adaptation, the following three papers overlap to provide a coherent picture: G. A. Bartholomew and J. B. Birdsell, "Ecology and the Protohominids," *American Anthropologist*, LV, No. 4 (1953); Marshall D. Sahlins, "The Origin of Society," *Scientific American*, CCIII, No. 3 (1960); and S. L. Washburn, "Tools and Human Evolution," *Scientific American*, CCIII, No. 3 (1960).

A recent and controversial effort to deal with behavior from a biological point of view is E. O. Wilson's *Sociobiology: The New Synthesis* (Cambridge: Belknap Press of Harvard University Press, 1975). Wilson's approach works fine for those creatures with which he is most familiar, but his attempt to extend the implications to the human realm are less successful precisely because he has failed to appreciate the nature of the cultural ecological niche.

Chapter Nine. The initial modest paper of R. A. Dart, remarkable for the furor which it touched off, is still worth reading: "*Australopithecus africanus:*

The Man-ape of South Africa," *Nature*, CXV (February 7, 1925). Professor Dart's personal involvement with Australopithecine research is depicted in *Adventures with the Missing Link* by R. A. Dart and Dennis Craig (New York: Harper and Brothers, 1959). The most comprehensive efforts to deal with the profusion of Plio-Pleistocene finds in Africa are by Glynn L. Isaac and E. R. McCown, eds. *Human Origins: Louis Leakey and the East African Evidence* (Menlo Park, California: Benjamin, 1976), and by Y. Coppens, F. C. Howell, G. L. Isaac and R. E. F. Leakey, eds. *Earliest Man and Environments in the Lake Rudolf Basin. Stratigraphy, Palaeoecology, and Evolution* (Chicago: University of Chicago Press, 1976). A crucial recent paper proving the contemporaneity of a late robust Australopithecine and a Pithecanthropine east of Lake Turkana, Kenya, is the one by R. E. F. Leakey and A. C. Walker, "*Australopithecus, Homo erectus*, and the single-species hypothesis," *Nature* (London), CCLXI (June 17, 1976).

Chapter Ten. For the Pithecanthropines, the standard reference against which all accounts are compared is Franz Weidenreich's "The Skull of *Sinanthropus pekinensis*," *Palaeontologia Sinica*, X (1943). Presenting a more historically oriented picture is G. H. R. von Koenigswald's "The Discovery of Early Man in Java and Southern China," in *Early Man in the Far East*, W. W. Howells, ed., Studies in Physical Anthropology, No. 1 (American Association of Physical Anthropologists, 1949).

Recent developments have been summarized by K. W. Butzer, G. L. Isaac, E. Butzer, and B. Isaac, eds. *After the Australopithecines: Stratigraphy, Ecology, and Culture Change in the Middle Pleistocene.* (The Hague: Mouton, 1975). The extensive Javanese finds of the last twenty years, as well as the earlier discoveries, are surveyed by Teuku Jacob, "The Pithecanthropines of Indonesia," *Bulletins et Memoires de de la Société d'Anthropologie de Paris*, II, série 13 (1975).

Chapter Eleven. Many if not most physical anthropologists prefer the approach to the Neanderthal problem represented in the writings of F. Clark Howell, for instance in "The Place of Neanderthal Man in Human Evolution," *American Journal of Physical Anthropology*, IX, No. 4 (1951); and "The Evolutionary Significance of Variation and Varieties of 'Neanderthal' Man," *Quarterly Review of Biology*, XXXII, No. 4 (1957). For a collection of papers generally in the traditional frame of reference, see *Hundert Jahre Neanderthaler: Neanderthal Centenary*, G. H. R. von Koenigswald, ed. (Utrecht: Kemink en Zoon, 1959).

A rather different view is presented by C. L. Brace in "Refocussing on the Neanderthal Problem," *American Anthropologist*, LXIV, No. 4 (1962).

Old views die hard, however, as can be shown in two recent papers by W. W. Howells, "Neanderthals: names, hypotheses, and scientific method," *American Anthropologist*, LXXVI, No. 1 (1974), and "Neanderthal man: facts and figures," *Yearbook of Physical Anthropology*, 1974, XVIII (1976).

Chapter Twelve. Comprehensive treatments of modern human physical development are represented by widely differing but mutually complementing approaches, for instance Theodosius Dobzhansky, *Mankind Evolving* (New Haven: Yale University Press, 1962); and Bernard G. Campbell, *Human Evolution: An Introduction to Man's Adaptation* (Chicago: Aldine Publishing Co., 1966).

A relatively standard treatment of contemporary human variation is seen in Carleton S. Coon's *The Living Races of Man* (New York: Alfred A. Knopf, 1965).

A less popular approach is taken by C. L. Brace in "A Non-racial Approach toward the Understanding of Human Diversity," in *The Concept of Race,* M. F. Ashley Montagu, ed. (New York: The Free Press of Glencoe, 1964); see also Part III in Brace and Montagu, *Human Evolution* (New York: The Macmillan Company, 1977).

Inde

112